Botley ar
Curdridge

A History of Two Hampshire Villages

Engraving of Botley by F N Shepherd and engraved by J Shury & Son for Robert Mudie's History of Hampshire, 1838

Hampshire Record Office:(FW78b)

Dennis Stokes

of the

Botley, Curdridge and Durley History Society

Published by:-

PENNY FARTHING GALLERY
21 The Square
Botley
Southampton
Hants
SO30 2EA
Tel. Botley (01489) 784185
penny_farthing@btconnect.com
www.pennyfarthinggallery.co.uk

Printed November 2007

Re-Printed January 2017

ISBN 978-0-9557571-0-5

The information in this book has been obtained from data housed at the *Botley Curdridge and Durley History Society* Archives; the Hampshire Record Office and local sources. We have endeavoured to verify the data provided. If, however, omissions or errors are noted, please notify the Publishers so that subsequent reprints can be updated.

Printed by:-

Ashford Print & Publishing Services

Unit 220, Fareham Reach

Fareham Road, Gosport

Hampshire, PO13 0PW

INTRODUCTION

Botley was described by William Cobbett in a letter he wrote in 1805 thus:-

'Botley is the most delightful village in the world. It has everything, in a village, that I love, and none of the things I hate. It is in a valley; the soil is rich, thickset with wood; the farms are small, the cottages neat; it has neither workhouse nor barber nor attorney nor justice of the peace, and, though last not least, it has no volunteers. There is no justice within six miles of us, and the barber comes three miles once a week to shave and cut hair! "Would I were poetical," I would write a poem in praise of Botley'.[*]

Curdridge was visited by Mary Russell Mitford and in her *'Recollections of a Literary Life'* she recalled visiting Cobbett's farm on the River Hamble:-

'….The fields [of Cobbett's Fairthorn Farm] lay along the Bursledon River, and might have been shown to a foreigner as a specimen of the richest and loveliest English scenery…..'

Botley and Curdridge are two adjoining and contrasting villages in south Hampshire midway between Southampton and Fareham and divided by the River Hamble.

Botley was a former market town with a wide main street, shops, houses and commercial premises at its centre and it still retains a bustling busy atmosphere. Curdridge on the other hand, has its buildings and farms spread over a wide area and although lacking a village centre and having three busy main roads through the parish, it maintains a relatively peaceful ambience.

This book has been written by the *Botley and Curdridge Local History Society* to record the history of these villages. It is a compilation of research undertaken both by villagers and *Botley and Curdridge Local History Society* members over many years. Their contribution to our knowledge of the history of the villages is immense. Many are now deceased but the researches and writings of the late Dr Alfred Pern; Mrs June Jones; Miss Vi Cooke; John Hogg; Tom Bishop; Arthur Tickner and Jack Tickner have been of particular value in writing this book.

---

[*] Brit.Lib. Add. MSS. 37853,f.177

We are also greatly indebted to the late Arthur Sidney Kilford, who recorded many images of Botley and Curdridge in the early part of the twentieth century. Kilford's nephew, Ken Gregory, was the recipient of most of the photographer's glass plate negatives and Ken wanted to ensure that the images were not lost and so donated them to the *Botley and Curdridge Local History Society*. It was Ken's wish that the plates should be held in safe keeping and also to provide an opportunity for villagers to view these images of their villages. The Society displayed the pictures at an exhibition in the Market Hall, Botley in March 2001 and the plates are now deposited with the Hampshire Record Office to ensure their continued conservation.

CONTENTS

CONTENTS (cont.)

EARLY HISTORY

*'From the west window in the drawing room at Botley Hill ' —a drawing by an artist
signed 'EAJ' (probably Elizabeth Jenkyns of Botley Hill House) c.1830.*

Hampshire Record Office (130M83/PZ13)

One of the earliest pieces of tangible evidence of Botley's ancient history are the remains of a Roman road which ran from Clausentum (Bitterne) to Portchester via present day Manor Farm. This road led to a ford which crossed the river Hamble just north of Curbridge Creek. The sites of a Roman building and a Roman pottery kiln in the grounds of Fairthorne Manor and the evidence of Roman buildings found on the Botley side of the river at the sewage works show that the settlement one would expect to find at such a river crossing did exist. This road would probably have been made between 50 and 100 AD.

It is quite possible, even if this site was not occupied by the Celts (Britain's oldest inhabitants), that the natural advantages of a river, which was shallow enough to be forded at low tide yet deep enough at high tide to accommodate sizeable vessels, would have commended itself to the maritime invaders from Northern Europe as a desirable place to colonise. This type of colonisation was prevalent in Southern Britain during the third and second centuries BC and these invaders eventually controlled Southern Britain driving the Celts westwards.

EARLY HISTORY

These intruders in their turn were defeated after many fierce battles by the Romans following their second invasion in 43 AD. After an occupation of about 400 years internal troubles of the Roman Empire caused the withdrawal of the Roman army and into the vacuum left by their departure, were drawn Angles and Saxons from the Continent who remained in control until the Norman Conquest of 1066. After the defeat of the Anglo-Saxons by William of Normandy, most of the landowners were replaced by Normans. The Domesday Book of 1087 says of Botley:-

"Ralph de Mortimer holds Botley and Cheping held it of King Edward. It was then as now assessed at 2 hides. Here are 6 ploughlands and 8 villeins and 4 borderers with 4 ploughlands, also a church, 4 servants, 2 mills worth 20s and 12 acres of meadow. There is no wood. Its value in the time of King Edward £10 afterwards was and is 100s."

The statement 'there is no wood' probably implied that the woodland was part of the Royal Forest of Bere and thus belonged to the Monarch.

The memory of Cheping and that of de Mortimer are recalled in the road names on the Four Acre Estate.

In 1236, one of de Mortimer's descendants was succeeded by someone who took the name of "John de Botele". [Lord of the Manor in about 1260 and Sheriff of Hampshire 1279]. John de Botele was a supporter of Henry III in defeating Simon de Montfort at Evesham in 1265 and was rewarded by the King to hold a Market and

Fair. The Charter proclaimed:-

1266-7 12 Feb.51 Henry III St Edmondsbury Grant and confirmation by the King to John de Botele and his heirs for ever of a market at his Manor of Botele weekly upon a Tuesday and a Fair there yearly for three days, that is on the vigil, the day and the morrow of All Saints Day unless the said markets and fairs shall be to the hurt of neighbouring markets and fairs: With a further grant of a free warren within the demesne lands of the Manor. Yet so that these lands shall not be within the bounds of the Kings Forest and so that no man may enter them as a fugitive or to take anything which pertains to warren without the licence and will of the same John upon forfeit of £10.

In 1304[1] Thomas de Botley, a descendent of John, granted the whole estate of Botley to the Bishop of Winchester probably under a trust for the endowment of the chapel of St. Elizabeth in Winchester. It remained in the possession of the Bishops until the dissolution of the monasteries in 1536.

Thomas Wriothesley, Earl of Southampton, obtained by Royal Grant many of the lands held by religious houses of Hampshire including Botley manor and church. He died in 1550 leaving a son and heir Henry, then a minor. Henry died in 1582 when the estate passed to his son Henry, the third Earl of Southampton, who died whilst on the King's service in 1624.

Thomas, his son and heir, became Lord High Treasurer in 1660 and held the manor until his death without male heirs in 1667. His elder daughter, Elizabeth, wife of

---

1. Victoria History of the Counties of England, Vol.3 pp 465-467

EARLY HISTORY

Edward Noel, first Earl of Gainsborough, inherited most of his property in Hampshire, including the manor of Botley. On the death of their only son without issue, Botley descended to their granddaughter Elizabeth, wife of William Bentinck, first Duke of Portland. It remained in her possession until 1775 when it was sold to the Rev. Richard Eyre, whose son succeeded him in 1823.

Ten years later the manor was purchased by James Warner of Steeple Court.

In Warner's time the area of the parish of Botley was much as it is today plus Botley Common which is now part of Hedge End. However the area along the Hamble River from Horsepool bridge in the north to Dock Copse in the south including Steeple Court and Marks Farm was part of Droxford parish until 1884, when it was transferred to Botley. In 1894 Hedge End became a separate parish.

A committee was formed to oversee the finance and building of a new parish church on land provided by James Warner. At a cost of £1720 the building commenced in 1835 and the church was consecrated on 22nd August 1836.

The two mills referred to in the Domesday Survey comprised two mills under one roof. A major reconstruction of the buildings was undertaken in 1770.

The mid 1800s saw many other changes in Botley. In 1829, a new weekly corn market opened in the square followed by a cattle market in 1830. James Warner provided the site for a Market Hall and partly financed its building which opened in 1848. The National School was built in 1855 and the Recreation Ground was purchased by public subscription in 1888.

The railway came to Botley (or more accurately – to Curdridge) in 1841. It was built by the London and Southampton Railway Company to provide a link to Portsmouth (via Gosport) from its London to Southampton line at Eastleigh. A branch line from Botley to Bishop's Waltham was opened to serve the large clay works and gas company there in 1863.

Wood, wood products and flour have been the principal exports of the village for many centuries being conveyed by barges to and from Botley Quay or the Mills. At the end of the nineteenth century strawberries became Botley's biggest industry with the fruit being exported by rail all over the country.

The Parish had a population in 1851 of 798 and an area of 1817 acres (735 hectares). The parish area changed in 1884 and again in 1894 when a large part of Botley Common became the southern part of Hedge End. Botley's population in the Census of 2001 was 5004 with an area of 2004 acres (811 hectares).

THE VILLAGE

Botley Village circa 1930 showing Botley Hill House (left foreground), Sherecroft (right foreground), the Square and the road to Southampton snaking away at the top of the picture.

Photo:Hampshire Record Office (63A04/B1/3/57)

THE VILLAGE

Botley Square looking east c.1905

It is probable that Botley developed where it is today during the medieval period to a point where the river crossing was less of a hazard. It is known that the river was bridged at Botley Mills with a timber construction as long ago as the sixteenth century. However, it is recorded that this bridge was frequently in need of repair and maintenance[2] and travellers would then have to wait for a low tide to ford the river before continuing their journey. It has often been reported that 14 public houses existed in the village to cater for the awaiting travellers but no records exist to confirm this assertion.

The construction of a brick bridge in 1797 opened up a safe highway to travellers and also increased the prosperity of the village.

The Universal British Directory of Trade for 1797 recorded that '....*Botley had lately emerged from obscurity and contempt, by the erection of a large brick built bridge over the river, the fording of which was a terror to travellers, and caused many to prefer a long and circuitous road by Winchester, rather than trust themselves to its uncertain and fluctuating depth'.*

Prior to this improvement in the river crossing, the population of the village in 1605 is estimated at 150 persons. (determined from church pew allocation in the parish records).[3]

Also in 1605, the pew allocation shows

2. HRO 5M53/1128/11   3. HRO 40M75/PR1

THE VILLAGE

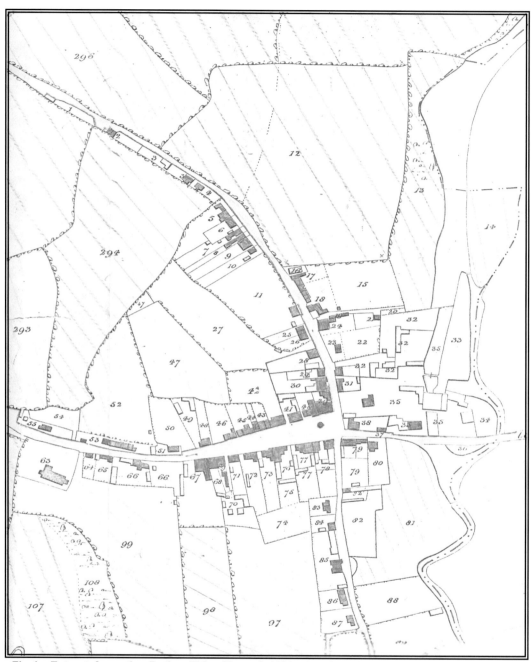

Fig.1—Extract from the Botley Tithe Map of 1839 showing the density of housing in the Botley village centre. The numbers refer to an associated Schedule listing owners, occupiers and land areas. Tithe Maps were produced following the Tithe Commutation Act 1836 to allow tithes to be commuted to a rent-charge.

Map:-Hampshire Record Office (40M75/PD1Extract)

THE VILLAGE

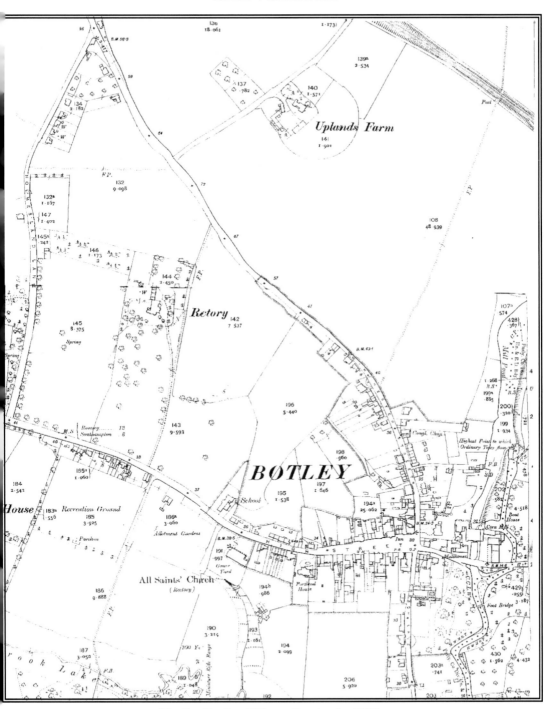

Fig.2—Botley Village Centre in 1909

Reproduced from 1909 Ordnance Survey map with the kind permission of the Ordnance Survey

THE VILLAGE

property and family names. Of the 32 properties listed, many are described as *'house in the street'* (present day High Street). Of those named, Maddoxford, Uplands, Heathhouse, Snakemoor, Steeplecourt, Botley Farm (now Manor Farm) and Catherine Wheel have survived into the twenty-first century. Another familiar name listed is of an Edward Markes residing in a *'Farm by the Church'* which is known today as Marks Farm.

Family names listed in 1605 which still exist in and around Botley today are - Owton (Houghton), Emery, Cozens (Cousins) and Abram (Abraham).

Later in 1680 a similar listing of pew allocation was prepared by the Rev. William

Hanbury and it shows 51 houses/farms with a population estimate of 216 but only eight family names survived from the 1605 record. In this 75 year period there is the emergence of now familiar place names such as Boorley Green, Horsepool, Braxells, the Bugle, Freegrounds and Pudbrook.

Public houses and shops have been a feature of Botley Square for many centuries. The first recorded hospice (Inn) was the Catherine Wheel in 1546 and the first recorded shop was in 1650 when Richard Cozen, a tenant of the Lord of the Manor, traded as a butcher in premises located on the north side of the Square.[4] By 1793 a

Biggs Saddler's shop on the south side of the High Street. c.1920

Photo:- Botley & Curdridge LHS (PH009)

4. HRO 5M53/397

THE VILLAGE

Above is Botley's original Post Office located on the south side of the High Street. It was severely damaged by fire in January 1914 and was relocated across the High Street next to the Bugle Inn in the premises of Walter Brock (below). When Brock sold his business, the Post Office reverted back to its original premises and finally, in the late 1980s, returned to its present position, within the Convenience Stores, again next to the Bugle Inn.

Photos: Arthur Kilford Collection (HRO 59A01/46 above & HRO 59A01/83)

THE VILLAGE

Elcock's Shoemaker Shop on the north side of the High Street. c.1910

Photo:- Arthur Kilford Collection (HRO 59A01/48)

Trade Directory shows there to have been three Public Houses (the Catherine Wheel, the Bugle and the Dolphin) and three shops (all of them mercers & grocers). One hundred years later the numbers had increased to 13 shops comprising 3 grocers, 3 bakers, 3 dressmakers, a butcher, draper, shoemaker and cycle agent. Additionally there were 4 public houses (the Dolphin, Botley Steam Brewery, the Bugle and the Three Horse Shoes) and a number of service trades - carpenter, blacksmith, coal dealer etc.

The built area of the village remained largely unaltered, from the end of the eighteenth century until the 1920s, which is partly illustrated by the maps Figs.1 & 2. In this period three significant buildings were constructed, the Church, Market Hall and the School, but these are relatively new compared to the majority of the buildings in the Square.

Botley House, east of Portland House, is thought to have comprised two Elizabethan cottages and the house was substantially altered in the 1760s when the Georgian front

THE VILLAGE

was added. The house is associated with the Guillaume family who lived here from 1782 to 1936. The Guillaumes were coal and timber merchants who owned a large part of Botley Quay. In the 1850s, William Edward Guillaume manufactured hoops from locally grown coppice wood.

The building west of the Market Hall is a sixteenth-century Grade 2 listed building with a modern extension on its eastern side. It was a butcher's shop owned by John Kingett in the early nineteenth century and in 1860 the property came into the ownership of William Bailey, a builder. He became the first superintendent of the Market Hall, a position later held by his son Frederick and grandson Arthur. The family served the village for nearly 100 years as builders, undertakers, ironmongers and Market Hall Superintendents[5]. Following the death of Arthur in the late 1960s, the property became an antique shop and this was followed by a succession of restaurants.

Between the restaurant and Botley House are eighteenth-century properties which include a former public house 'The Three Horse Shoes'. Next to these is the 'Pennyfarthing Gallery'. The Pennyfarthing derives its name from its former premises where the business started 30 years ago in Arthur Kilford's shop at No. 31 High Street, which had been a cycle shop at the beginning of the twentieth century.

High Street looking east with the Blacksmith's Forge on the left hand side c.1920

Photo:- Hampshire Record Office (63A04/B1/3/16)

5. HRO 60A01

THE VILLAGE

A newer building is Portland House or Villa, as it was first known, which was built c.1866. It has been the home to two of Botley's well known families of the twentieth century – the widow of the first Dr Pern and the Maffey family. One of its first residents was William Harding who, in the 1885 General Election, used the house as the Conservative Committee Room which became a principal target from rioters during the infamous 'Botley Riots'.

Next to Portland House is the former cottage and shop of Arthur Kilford. The eighteenth-century cottage to which the shop was added in the late nineteenth century was previously owned by James Warner, father of James Warner, Lord of the Manor of Botley. Warner was listed as a 'Rake Maker' and the Tithe Map Schedule of 1839 shows the property to be *'house, buildings and Cooper's shop'*. At the end of the nineteenth century the Kilford family resided here and Arthur Phillip Kilford ran various businesses including petrol agent, stationer, cycle sales and repairs and hairdresser. It was here that his son Arthur Sidney Kilford continued the business and started his photographic hobby. The adjoining buildings were built as stables in the 1780s and were converted into cottages

High Street looking west c.1914. Kilford's shop on the left

Photo:-Arthur Kilford Collection (HRO 59A01/113)

THE VILLAGE

in the mid nineteenth century.

Most of the shops and houses on the north side of the Square are of an eighteenth-century date, the exception being those to the east of Warner Mews which were built in 1969. Forge Cottage is an early nineteenth-century grade 2 listed building in which several blacksmiths traded. William Aslett lived here until his death in the mid 1830s when his wife Hannah appeared to continue the business. Samuel Bastable acquired the premises and his family continued to trade as blacksmiths until the late 1930s.

The population of the village very gradually increased over this period from 614 in 1801 to 1166 in 1921. The first significant expansion was in Winchester Street in 1922 when houses were built on the eastern side. It was after the Second World War that housing and population increased four fold in 30 years. In 1950 the Four Acre Estate was built followed by the Pern Drive and Mortimer Road developments in the 1960s. Boorley Green continued to infill and in the late 70s, the Holmesland and King's Copse estates were built. The population of Botley had increased to 5166 in 2001.

Dan Bell's coal yard on the banks of the river c.1925. Today it is the site of Hamblewood Court.

Photo:- Arthur Kilford Collection (HRO 59A01/101)

THE VILLAGE

View of the village looking west. c1908

Photo:- Hampshire Record Office (63A04/B1/3/17)

Botley Village looking east. 1907. Note the sign of the Three Horse Shoes Public House on the right of this picture.

Photo:- Hampshire Record Office (63A04/B1/3/12)

THE VILLAGE

High Street looking west with the Church War Memorial on the left . The school is partly hidden by a cottage which was demolished in the 1930s.

Photo:- Botley and Curdridge LHS (PH554)

Mill Hill c.1914

Photo:- Botley & Curdridge LHS (PH005)

THE VILLAGE - WINCHESTER STREET

**The Brewery Bar formerly Edwards' Brewery. The tenant of the Brewery Bar,
William Plummer is seen on the left. c.1915**

Photo:- Botley & Curdridge LHS (PH558)

Winchester Street leads north from the High Street. Until the early 1800s, the street contained only a few houses and tradesmen but remained a track through Boorley Green ending in a maze of tracks on Horton Heath.

The road contains one of the oldest houses in the village, the jettied property at No. 8 built in 1610.

William Cobbett, who wanted to provide a better access to market towns, was responsible for the construction of the turnpike road between Winchester and Gosport in 1809. Thus a direct road to Winchester was provided rather than the previous route via Bishop's Waltham.

At about this time the Chapel was constructed which was later to become the Congregational Church. Following the amalgamation of the Congregational and Presbyterian Churches of England in 1972, it became the United Reform Church but very shortly afterwards it was demolished and two garages now occupy the site.

In 1840, as the railway was being constructed between Bishopstoke and Fareham, Winchester Street was realigned to cross the railway track at Boorley Green.

The first shop in Winchester Street listed in Trade Directories appears to be a James Houghton, a butcher and baker in 1844. Edwards' Brewery, later to become the Brewery Bar, was established in the 1850s.

THE VILLAGE - WINCHESTER STREET

Winchester Street looking south. c.1910

Photo:- Botley & Curdridge LHS (PH031)

Winchester Street looking north. c.1910

Photo:-Hampshire Record Office (63A04/B1/3/31)

THE VILLAGE - WINCHESTER STREET

Winchester Street looking south showing the Chapel. c.1900

Photo:-Botley & Curdridge LHS (CPIC0107)

Hawkins Grocery Store on the west side of Winchester Street. c.1910

Photo:-Arthur Kilford Collection (HRO 59A01/42)

THE VILLAGE - CHURCH LANE

Church Lane runs south from the High Street and today it leads to the old Church and Manor Farm and connects with Brook Lane.

The area between Steeplecourt and Marks Farm and eastwards to the river was a detached part of the Parish of Droxford. It was ceded to Botley by order of the Local Government Board in 1884.

Prior to 1884, the Lane existed only as far as Horsepool bridge by Botley Quay. However, it was still the principal route for pedestrians on their way to worship at the former Parish Church. They would make their way down the lane and then take the Church Path (now curiously called 'Lovers Lane') over the stream by Burgessland and, via footpaths, to the Church.

Entering Church Lane from the Square two very historic buildings stand opposite one another. On one corner is a building known for over 450 years as the Catherine Wheel and on the left hand side is a building which is probably medieval in origin. Its smoke blackened (internal) roof timbers indicate an 'open hall' construction. In the late eighteenth and early nineteenth century, it

Ivy Cottage in Church Lane with the Malthouse on the right

Photo:-Arthur Kilford Collection (HRO 59A01/43)

THE VILLAGE - CHURCH LANE

became a public house and known as 'The Gate Hangs High'. It is said that a sign of a miniature five barred gate hung outside with the words:

This gate hangs high and hinders none.
Refresh and pay and travel on.

Beyond this building are the stables of William Cobbett's house when he resided in Botley in the early nineteenth century. Opposite is the Malthouse, a building formerly used to process malt from barley. Next door is Ivy Cottage and opposite, the boundary wall of Cobbett's Botley House bows inwards and would have allowed for the turning of a horse and carriage.

Beyond the Parish Quay and over the Horsepool bridge is Steeple Court, an Elizabethan manor house and a former residence of some notable Botley people, including James Warner, Admiral Colomb and the members of the Jenkyns family.

Church Lane looking north

Photo:-Botley & Curdridge LHS (PH017)

THE VILLAGE - CATHERINE WHEEL

The Catherine Wheel c.1910

Photo:-.Botley & Curdridge LHS (PH021)

The first record of the Catherine Wheel is in the 'Rentals for the Manor of Botley' of 1546 in which it states *'Holds freehold a certain hospice* [meaning guest house or ale house] *called The Katerine Whele. Rent by customary services set forth annually by shoe money'.*[6] It is thought that this service was to provide horseshoes to the Lord of the Manor (Sir Thomas Wriothesley) in lieu of monetary rent. The Catherine Wheel was mentioned in the seventeenth- century parish registers and it was probably the first public house in Botley. It was listed in early nineteenth-century Trade Directories as one of several public houses in the Square. Today you can see the outline of a cellar entrance to the left of the shop entrance where barrels were delivered.

The name originates from St Catherine of Alexandra. It is said that Catherine converted 50 heathen philosophers to Christianity and for this she was condemned to die on a wheel armed with knives, saws and nails. She was however rescued from this wheel and beheaded. Our picture shows the sign of the Wheel was suspended from a bracket prior to renovations in 1980, when it was then affixed to the wall.

In 1882 the Catherine Wheel became available for sale and it was acquired by the Church of England Temperance Society with major contributions from Mrs Lee the Rector's wife and Mr Henry Jenkyns

6 HRO 11M59/158819/8 also H G Barstow - *Manor Rentals of Botley 1546/7*

THE VILLAGE - CATHERINE WHEEL

who later became Sir Henry Jenkyns of Botley Hill House. Jenkyns and the Rector, John Morley Lee, rebuilt and enlarged the former public house to create a coffee house and temperance hotel. The accommodation provided bedrooms for hire; a bar selling non-alcoholic beverages and food; rooms for lectures and public meetings and rooms for the Botley Institute and also a Reading Room library. The latter contained daily and weekly papers and a lending library[7].

The house was supported largely by the generosity of Canon Lee and when he died in 1903 the incumbency passed to the Reverend Osborne. Osborne however was unable for financial reasons to continue to support the house in the same way as Canon Lee. He thus invited principal members of the community to join him in forming a committee to help him manage the house. The committee known initially as the Temperance Hotel Committee and then the Catherine Wheel Committee, found it difficult to keep the Hotel viable. In the minutes of the first meeting of the Committee in September 1903 it was noted *'A discussion took place as to why the house had failed financially'.*

One of the remedies proposed was to appoint a manager and consequently a Mr Lyne was given the post. For the next few years the Hotel managed to support itself financially and by 1916 the first recorded donation, of £18, was given to the church to defray the cost of black-out curtains. The Committee continued to increase its profits and provided further donations to the church and the school.

Also with improvements to their own premises and the installation of a gas supply in 1925 it enabled the 'Wheel' to provide cookery classes, dentistry and medical welfare services. In 1932, the Institute had outgrown the rooms it occupied and the Catherine Wheel committee provided a sum of £423 to erect the Institute building at the rear of its premises. Electricity was installed in 1935 to the Catherine Wheel and to the Institute building free of cost to the Institute.

During the Second World War the Wheel was kept in good use for the accommodation of troops and evacuees.

The business continued to grow under the management of the committee and Mr Bert Earwicker who had been appointed manager in 1929. Mr Earwicker retired in 1963 and it was at this point that the committee decided that the purpose for which the house was originally used no longer existed. And so the Catherine Wheel Committee was disbanded and its financial assets of £3000 distributed to all the organisations of the village.

The new tenants were a Mr and Mrs Taylor, long term residents of the village, and the Catherine Wheel continued to prosper as a grocery and sweet shop. In 1980 it was bought by a Mr Fagg and converted to a bakery and it remained a very popular bread and cake shop until its closure in March, 2003.

The building was renovated in 2004 to create flats and two retail outlets. Sadly the name 'Catherine Wheel' has disappeared.

7. HRO 40M75/PK3

THE VILLAGE - MAFFEYS

Maffeys Drapery shop on the corner of the High Street and Winchester Street c.1915

Photo — Botley & Curdridge LHS (PH059)

Older villagers may recall the time when Botley contained the shops necessary to provide for nearly all of their needs. Until the late 1970s Botley village centre had shops providing groceries, meat, bread, confectionery, petrol, greengroceries, clothes, drapery, ironmongery, a pharmacy, Post Office and Bank etc. None of the old established businesses such as Maffeys, Gibsons, Elcocks, Roxburgh & Scivier, the Catherine Wheel, Lloyds Bank and Lewrys the Butcher exist today.

One business that endured from before the first World War until well after the Second World War was Maffeys.

Joseph Maffey was born at Idmeston in Wiltshire in 1845. He and his family moved to Pink Mead in Curdridge in 1870 and seven years later, Joseph acquired for his sons, George and Ernest, Marsh's Stores standing on the corner of the High Street and Winchester Street. After his marriage George left the district and Ernest was joined by his younger brother Arthur (1881-1967).

On the death of Mr Walter Brock, of the

THE VILLAGE - MAFFEYS

Maffey's Grocery shop next to the Bugle c.1930

Photo:- Arthur Kilford Collection (HRO 59A01/119)

'Cash Stores and Post Office' next to the Bugle Inn, the Maffeys acquired the shop and reopened it as a grocery store.

The firm of Messrs J Maffey and Sons became widely known in southern Hampshire and was later formed into a limited company.

Ernest Maffey was born in 1870 and he and his wife Mary Botting had 6 daughters and 2 sons and lived in the High Street at Portland House. He died in 1948 and four of their daughters were to live into their nineties. Indeed Florence Ethel lived to over one hundred years old.

Arthur and his family of two daughters lived at *Hindon* in Winchester Street. (Hindon was the village name of his birthplace in Wiltshire).

With the growth of out of town shopping, the demand for local shops fell and the two Maffey shops closed in the 1970s.

The last of Ernest's daughters, Florence Ethel died in 2002 and much of the Maffey estate was bequeathed to the church which has provided a Rectory and helped to fund a new church extension.

Florence Ethel Maffey on her 100th birthday, 29th September, 1999.

Photo: By kind permission of Beryl Cook

THE VILLAGE - MAFFEYS

Maffeys delivery cart in the High Street c.1920

Photo:- Arthur Kilford Collection (HRO 59A01/221)

THE VILLAGE - LEWRYS

Lewrys Butchers shop, High Street c.1910

Photo:- Arthur Kilford Collection (HRO 59A01/125)

Alfred John Lewry was born in 1853 at Pyecombe in Sussex.

He came to Botley and in 1875 started trading in the Market Square as a butcher with a small cash capital. By the turn of the century the business thrived and with his sons, William, Percival and Cecil, he opened branches in Bursledon and Shedfield.

Alfred took up farming in the 1880s and at one time had a total holding of 40 acres in Botley and Hedge End. He joined the Botley and South Hants Farmers Club in 1876 and for 50 years was a member of the Ancient Order of Foresters. Alfred retired from the business and in 1916 he became Clerk to Botley Parish Council, a trustee of the Market Hall, and a life committee man of the Botley Institute. He died in July 1931 and is buried in Botley's churchyard.

His son, William, and then grandson, Horace, continued the business throughout most of the twentieth century.

Peter Hillier became manager of the shop in the 1970s having worked for the Lewry family since he was 14 years old. Then in 1979 he acquired the business and it was successfully run by Peter and then by his son Nick until its closure in 2012.

THE VILLAGE - MARKET

Botley Market Hall c.1920

Botley had a market as long ago as 1226 when Henry III granted a Royal Warrant to John de Botele to hold a weekly market and an annual fair. It appears that the market continued for well over 500 years until it came to an end in the latter part of the eighteenth century.

James Warner of Steeple Court, a local farmer and landowner, and soon to become the Lord of the Manor of Botley, resurrected the market in 1829 as a corn market and the following year a cattle market.

According to the *Hampshire Chronicle*, the market was very successful and on the opening of the cattle market on the 7th April 1830, it was reported that '*800 sheep & lambs were penned and there was also a good supply of horses, horned cattle and pigs*'.

At the close of the market, the farmers would retire to the Dolphin Hotel for a dinner. One of the founders of the market was Sir Raymond Jarvis of Fair Oak who, in gratitude for the hospitality he received from

THE VILLAGE - MARKET

the farmers on market day, presented a large porcelain jug which he promised to fill with punch so long as he should be able to attend the Botley Cattle Market. Many toasts were drunk and songs sung. Often the dinner would be finished with a special fruit pudding and so popular was this dessert that it became known as the 'Botley Pudding'.

James Warner wanted a permanent administration centre for the farmers and so

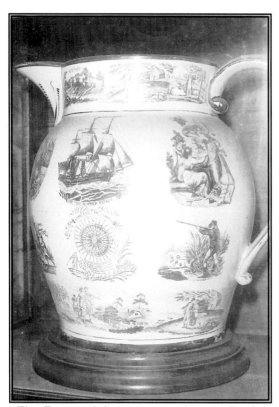

The Farmers' Jug presented to the Botley Farmers' Club by Sir Raymond Jarvis. Now deposited with the Hampshire Museum Service

Photo—Botley & Curdridge LHS(PH344)

he purchased the cottage of John Wiltshire, a cordwainer and in 1848, Warner had the Market House built on the site for £700 which was mainly funded by him and partly by subscription from the persons using the market, and so it is one of the more recent buildings in the Square.

The imposing building was much as we see it today but without the clock tower. Inside an internal door connected the Hall to the Dolphin Hotel, but in 1889 it was locked when it was found that a Licensing Act prohibited the use of an internal communication between a licensed and unlicensed premises used for public entertainment. The liability to a penalty of £10 caused the door to be bricked up in 1896.[8]

James Warner died in 1858 and the Market Hall passed to his son, William. William and the trustees of his father's will knew that it had been the intention of James Warner to lease the Market Hall for a long period at low rent to the Farmers for the benefit of the market. So in September 1858, William Warner leased the Hall to the Farmers for 1000 years at a nominal rent of one shilling a year.

Twenty six years later, the Hall came into public ownership when the Warner family offered the hall and the yard behind it for sale for £150. It was bought jointly by the Farmers and the people of Botley. A Deed of Trust was prepared on the 25th August 1884 which nominated four members of the Farmers' Club and four from the Vestry to be appointed as Trustees.

8. HRO 60A01

THE VILLAGE - MARKET

To help make the building pay for itself, one proposal was to install a weighbridge outside the front of the Hall to assist in the levying of market tolls. Its cost and installation amounted to £150. A question of how this cost was to be funded was again resolved by the Warner family who, most generously, offered to pay costs and to lease the weighbridge to the Trustees for £5 per annum.

In its early years, the Hall was let out to various organisations including the Hampshire Volunteer Regiment who surprisingly, kept their armoury in the hall and magazine in the yard! Other early lettings included a gymnastics club, woodwork classes and dairy demonstrations by the Government's Technical Education Committee.

William Bailey had been appointed as Superintendent of the Market Hall in 1884 and his duties included cleaning, maintenance, collection of market and weighbridge tolls and letting the Hall. The position of Superintendent was to be held by three generations of the Bailey family which spanned 72 continuous years of service.

To celebrate the Diamond Jubilee of the reign of Queen Victoria in 1897, the clock tower was added. Interestingly, the clock is the only part of the Market Hall owned and maintained by the Parish Council.

With improved transport, the bigger markets of Winchester and Southampton became more attractive and brought about the demise of Botley Market and it closed at the turn of the century.

The Market Hall has been used to house many of the village's historical artefacts, including the Farmers' Jug, previously mentioned, an historic canoe and the Hall's original chandelier. All of these items are now deposited with local museums.

During the last war, the Hall was used as a reception centre for bombed out refugees from Southampton and Portsmouth and then it was commandeered by the Home Guard.

After the war there was a desperate need to modernise the Hall but the nature of the constitution was such that the Trustees were unable to obtain a financial grant for the work. It was therefore resolved to seek advice from the Charity Commission who recommended that the Hall be administered by a management committee of five elected members and a representative from all the organisations using the hall. This new administration took effect on 28th December 1967. Money was raised and the building was enlarged to include improved kitchen and toilet facilities and additional meeting rooms.

Local Government and lottery grants have enabled further modernisation of the Hall in 2004 to 2006 by the implementation of acoustic panelling to the ceiling, introduction of a public address and hearing loop system, provision of improved disabled access and changes to improve the visual aspect of the building.

THE VILLAGE - MARKET

The Hall has provided a self financing facility for the villagers of Botley for which we owe a debt of gratitude to all those trustees, managers, caretakers and others, who for over 150 years, have mostly provided their services for nothing. But, above all, we should be forever grateful to the Warner family, particularly James Warner, for he has given a building of style and character which enhances the village and is of immense value to the villagers.

THE VILLAGE - MARKET HALL - HORTICULTURAL SHOWS

There has been a horticultural show at Botley Market Hall nearly every year since the Hall was built in 1848.

The Show was first organised by the Botley and South Hants Farmers' Club, a club formed by James Warner, Lord of the Manor of Botley. During the early years the Show took the form of 'An Annual Root Show' and ploughing competitions at a local farm. Classes for the show typically included 'Ten acres of Swedes', 'Six acres of Turnips' and 'Two acres of Mangold Wurtzels'. Exhibits in the Hall included 'Six best shaped Swedes,' 'Six heaviest stubble turnips' and 'Four heaviest kohl rabi' etc. Prizes ranged from £6 for the field exhibit of 10 acres of Swedes to 5 shillings (25p) for heaviest turnips. The prize money was donated by neighbouring landowners including Thomas Chamberlayne of Cranbury Park and Sir Edward Butler of Harefield House.

The Root Show was held in late November and a flower show was also held in the Market Hall in September.

Later the Show was arranged by the Botley Farmers' Growmore Club. The Government encouraged the formation of local Growmore Clubs during World War II. Its aim was to enable farmers and their workers to meet together to discuss improvement in all aspects of farming technology and to maximise food production.

Botley's Growmore Club was formed on 2nd December 1942 and included farmers from West End, Hedge End, Curdridge and Botley. Its first Chairman was Mr Harold Yates.

One of its first shows after the war described the show as 'Annual Exhibition of Pulled Roots, Apples, Corn and Table Poultry'.

In the 1960s, the Show was hosted by the Botley Rose and Sweet Pea Society followed by the Botley Show Committee and then, in 1997, by the Botley Gardening Club.

Botley & South Hants Farmers' Club Show held in the Market Hall c.1910

Photo:- Arthur Kilford Collection (HRO 59A01/204)

THE VILLAGE - MARKET HALL - HORTICULTURAL SHOWS

Botley & South Hants Farmers' Club Show held in the Market Hall c.1910

Photo:-Botley & Curdridge LHS (CPIC0088)

Botley Gardening Club Show held in the Market Hall. 2005

Photo:- DH Stokes

ALL SAINTS CHURCH

Botley Church looking southeast c.1910.

Photo:- Arthur Kilford Collection (HRO 59A01/10)

There has been a place of worship in Botley for at least 1000 years. In King William's Domesday Book of 1086 a part of the entry for Botley reads - *"here is a church"*, whilst the list of Rectors of the Parish dates from 1282.

The present church of All Saints was built in 1835-36 and supersedes the Old Parish Church, part of which is still standing, about half a mile to the south of the present village.

There were several reasons for replacing the Old Church. Firstly, it became increasingly expensive to keep in good repair. It was too small for the growing population (722 at the 1831 census) and the village had developed some distance from the church where the River Hamble had become easier to cross.

Another reason for building a new church was, in the words of a contemporary writer, *'A Dissenting Chapel had been built in Winchester Street and plans were afoot for increasing its seating capacity. A goodly*

ALL SAINTS CHURCH

number of Parishioners had started to attend Divine Service at the Chapel rather than face the long walk to the old church'. In those days Church Lane did not extend beyond the Parish Quay, and the route to be taken was by the Church Path, over which all corpses were carried to the grave, across open fields and four stiles, which was not only inconvenient but *'scarcely decent for females to climb over'*, as a writer of those times declared.

At the end of the eighteenth century the church was badly damaged by a fallen tree.

A committee comprising the Rector and six of the most influential men in the village was formed to raise funds for the building of a new church. In this they were successful, for aided by a grant from the *'Incorporated Society for Promoting the Enlargement, Building and Repair of Churches'* they soon had enough funds to begin the building.

The committee for building the new church comprised the Rector (Rev Richard Baker) as Chairman, John Jenkyns, a London lawyer who lived at Botley Hill, William Wells who managed Jenkyns estate and other prominent Botley villagers.[9]

Architects were invited to submit plans, and the design most favoured by the Committee was that produced by a Mr James Wild, who quoted a cost of £1,785. In the opinion of some people the design was somewhat plain and uninteresting but this may in part be attributed to the fact that the architect soon found himself running into trouble with the costs. To try and keep within Contract Price, many of the *'Frills and Fancy Bits'* had to be omitted.

The Rev Richard Baker was soon to upset other members of the committee; disagreeing with the selected architect and the escalating cost of the design and then objecting to the appointment of local builders, Newman, Wilkins and Gurman to construct the church. Baker stormed out of the selection meeting saying *'I will have nothing to do either directly or indirectly in sanctioning the foundation and erection of my parish church by such persons as Newman and Wilkins, men of destructive principles to the constitution of the church and State in this country and hope you (the committee) can satisfy your conscience or reconcile your own principles with supporting such men in the building of a church…'*

John Jenkyns took over the Chairmanship of the Building Committee but still the Rector was critical of the actions of the committee – he was upset at not being consulted on the arrangements for the consecration of laying the foundation stone nor for the consecration of the Church although he did officiate under the Bishop of Winchester. He complained that the builders were working on the Sabbath day and that the pulpit was too small and in the wrong place.

The site having been given by Mr James Warner, Lord of the Manor, the foundation stone was laid on 11th June 1835. The occasion was made one of the greatest joy and jollification. At that time the village had a band which provided accompaniment for

9.HRO 44M80

ALL SAINTS CHURCH

hymns at the ceremony. Afterwards the Clergy and Congregation moved in slow procession to the adjoining field, where gaily striped tents had been erected and a Fair provided, the proceeds from these events going towards the Church Building Fund. Plum cakes were ordered from three Botley bakers for the occasion and we know that 600 cakes from Mr Benjamin Bye cost £1-12s-0d (£1.60).

The building of the church went ahead and the Consecration Ceremony took place on 22nd August 1836, at which there was a congregation of 700 (including 54 Clergy), although the church was only designed to seat 500.

The church was built in the early Gothic or Lancet style. The walls were faced with white Southampton bricks, the stone around the doors and windows being Bath Stone. As originally built, the church was a rectangular structure with a small vestry adjoining the East end and a porchway over the West Door, with the Tower projecting from the Northwest Corner.[10]

A gallery which was built across the West end of the Nave was reached from the tower. The faint outline of the blocked-up doorway can still be seen. When the North Aisle was built the gallery was removed.

The Tower

There are six bells housed in the tower. Three were brought from the former church. Two of these date from c1420 (numbered 4 and 6) and were cast at Wokingham and a third (number 5) was recast in 1920. Three new bells (numbered 1 to 3) were cast at

Whitechapel in 2000 to celebrate the new millennium.

The Clock

The clock was originally on William Cobbett's residence which was called "the Great House" until its demolition and was then transferred to the stable buildings which still exist in Church Lane. Cobbett was Botley's famous radical writer and author of *Rural Rides*, who will be the subject of a later chapter. The date 1836 on the clock face is the date of completion of the church, the clock itself being much older. It is an early open frame type, made by John May of Southampton and has a single strike.

It was repaired by Padbury in 1863 and by G H Bell in 1953. The clock was later converted to an electrical winding system by the Midland Clock Works, Derby.

The North Aisle

The North Aisle, which was added in 1892, filled in the space between the Organ housing and the Tower. The piers are made of oak from the Broadlands Estate, Romsey, with wooden arcading, a rarity met within only two other churches in Hampshire. Dormer windows were fitted in the roof as well as a stone balustrade which somewhat improved the appearance of the North side. This aisle was made into a War Memorial Chapel in 1949.

ALL SAINTS CHURCH

Organ

The organ housing was built in 1852 to accommodate the organ made by Walker of London. This instrument, which replaced a barrel organ, cost £140. It was enlarged in 1883 and again in 1892.

Chancel

The Chancel and Priest's Vestry were added in 1859. The Choir Vestry behind the Chancel was built in 1844. Extensive changes in the layout of the Chancel took place in 1955, the choir stalls were placed in the nave and the Communion Rails were moved out to the Chancel Arch. A new Altar was presented in memory of the Rev G Salwey, Rector of Botley 1919-1946, the old Altar being placed in the Old Church. The carved Reredos, which was installed in 1886, was removed and presented to a church in Wales which had no decoration of any kind. At this time the Pulpit was moved from the South side of the Chancel arch to the North side.

Recumbent Figure

The recumbent figure against the South wall, which was removed from the Old Church is thought to be that of John de Botele. He was a kinsman of the famous William of Wyckham, Bishop of Winchester. It will be seen that the remains of the animal at the feet of the figure is facing the "wrong way" i.e. towards the wall. Old records tell us that the figure had been against the South wall in the Old Church as well. Now did the sculptor make a mistake, or had the figure, at some time been against another wall?

Font

The Font which was removed from the Old Church has a strange history. It is said to have been dug up in a field near Fairthorne in about 1740, but when and for what reason it was buried there is not known. This old Font must be quite unique, the motif of arches, in one section intertwining, is said by some to be Saxon, although the general opinion of the experts is that it is probably early Norman.

The mason who did the sculpting may have been very deficient in skill for the carving seems to be quite crude. This indeed seems to have been its particular charm. There can surely be few less inhibited carvings of this type in existence. No two sections are anywhere near identical. The font was originally tub shaped but when found it was seen to be damaged at the base, and was later re-cut to its present shape. A font of similar design of arches exists in St. Martin's Church in Canterbury.

Stained Glass Windows

The East window, given by Canon and Mrs Lee, in memory of both their fathers, depicts the 23rd Psalm.

The four windows in the south wall are:-

1. In memory of Admiral C J Rowley and Major P Rowley of Holmesland.

2. In memory of Eleanor Maria Trench.

ALL SAINTS CHURCH

All Saints Church Font

Photo:- Arthur Kilford Collection (HRO 59A01/30)

3. The Warner window, in memory of James and Eleanor Warner of Steeple Court.

4. The Jenkyns memorial window.

The latter was consecrated on the 14th July 1984 in memory of the Jenkyns family, late of Botley Hill, Curdridge and Steeple Court, Botley. With the death of Major Robert Jenkyns in 1981 there came to an end a period of 150 years during which the family lived here.

The window was designed and largely made by Mr John Hayward. The theme suggests not only a family tree but a tree bearing the seven life giving sacraments as its fruit against a background of local associations.

The West window was given by the Lee family in memory of Canon and Mrs Lee. Canon Morley Lee was Rector of Botley from 1854 to 1903.

One of the stained glass windows in the North wall was given by the Pern family in memory of Dr Pern, who died in 1970, and is unique in that it depicts a likeness of the Doctor. It was Dr Pern's proud assertion that Botley had only two doctors, and two People's Wardens in nearly one hundred

ALL SAINTS CHURCH

The interior of All Saints Church showing the font, gas lighting and the Reredos decoration at the rear of the Chancel. c.1908

Photo: Hampshire Record Office (63A04/B1/3/5)

that Botley had only two doctors, and two People's Wardens in nearly one hundred years—his father and himself.

Narthex and Extension

The Narthex across the whole width of the West end was added in 1895. It was demolished in 2007 and replaced by an extension to provide meeting rooms, kitchen facilities, toilets and a reception area.

Church Room

The Church Room at the East end was added in 1967

War Memorial

The War Memorial, dedicated in 1921 commemorates the names of thirty-three men of Botley who gave their lives in the 1914-1918 war. An additional twelve names were added after the 1939-1945 war.

The churchyard has been extended southwards twice, in 1885 and 1935, and it

ALL SAINTS CHURCH

is anticipated that a new burial ground will become necessary in the near future.

Many prominent Botley residents have found their last resting place in the churchyard including Reverend Richard Baker (Rector 1803-1854) and Reverend John Morley-Lee (Rector 1854-1903) and the Admirals Aynsley, Barry, Colomb, Rowley and Sparshott.

At one time a row of old elm trees bordered the churchyard and the road. Unfortunately they became diseased and dangerous and had to be felled in 1915.

A new church extension was constructed in 2007 to provide offices, a Rural Discovery Centre, Library and an IT suite. A Service of Celebration and Dedication of the new extension took place on 22nd September 2007.

All Saints Church, Botley with new Church Extension. September 2007

Photo:-DH Stokes

ALL SAINTS CHURCH - RECTORIES

Eighteenth-century Rectory built near to St Bartholomew's Church in Church Lane. c.1920

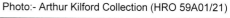

Photo:- Arthur Kilford Collection (HRO 59A01/21)

Nineteenth-century Rectory erected following the construction of the new church in 1836. The Rectory was demolished in the 1980s when Jenkyns Close was built.

Photo:- Arthur Kilford Collection (HRO 59A01/44)

ST BARTHOLOMEW'S CHURCH

Half a mile to the south of the village centre stand the remains of the old parish church. It was built in the thirteenth century and replaced churches that had existed there since Saxon times. The church is dedicated to All Saints but is known locally as St. Bartholomews.

The church was a long and narrow building consisting of a nave and chancel approximately 80 feet long and 22 feet wide externally.

The entrance to the church was from the north by a small porch and a round headed Norman doorway.

When built the church must have been very dimly lit with narrow lancet windows, initially without glass and limited in number.

In the first two decades of the eighteenth century, the Rector of Botley, the Rev. Joseph Walton attempted to brighten up the church. In the parish register he wrote *'that as the chancel was so dark and gloomy he and his friends at his request put in two large new windows'*. He also introduced an organ on the south side of the chancel and provided seats there *'for the children to sing'*.[11]

St Bartholomew's Church near Manor Farm Country park. c.1908

Photo:- Arthur Kilford Collection (HRO 59A01/127)

11. HRO 40M75/PV1

ST BARTHOLOMEW'S CHURCH

At a meeting in 1818 it was recorded that the Vestry should consider rendering the church *'decent, warm and commodious'*. It was resolved that William Othen *'shall do up the steeple end round with bricks, and brick and cast the inside and colour it on the outside for the sum of eight pounds'*.

It was also decided to ask Mr Fielder for an estimate for *'moving the pulpit and desk, putting in a staircase to the gallery and removing the seats and doing up the entrance thereto'*.

Seven years later in 1825, the Vestry again discussed repairs to the church and sought to provide a Vestry room by converting the church porch. The resolution was carried by a majority vote but it was recorded that Robert Gater, Benjamin Bye and Robert Chandler protested against the decision. Their reason for opposition was that there should be no further expenditure on the repair of the church but building a new church must be considered.

However shortly after the Vestry Room had been erected, the church was severely damaged by the fall of a tree and became so dilapidated that it was described as *'nothing more than a heap of ruins'*

It was said that this shameful condition of the church was partly due to its age and partly to the neglect of several generations who had failed to make adequate provision for its proper maintenance and repair.

When the new church was finally built in the High Street in 1836, the former church became neglected but through the efforts of James Warner, Lord of the Manor and his sisters, a complete renovation of the church was undertaken in 1857. The nave was dismantled and a west wall built using the stone from the demolished nave, and a partly late twelfth–century doorway incorporated in the new wall. An oak turret covered in tiles was constructed to house a single bell.

It was said that the Rector planted two shrubs at the corner of where the nave ended *'as a sort of*

Sketch of St. Bartholomew's Church how it may have looked at the start of the 19th Century by Archdeacon Fearon

From 'Some Hampshire Churches' Published by G F Wilson Co Ltd
(Copy held by Botley & Curdridge LHS)

ST BARTHOLOMEW'S CHURCH

record' but there is now no trace of these.

The church has not been used for regular worship since 1836 and was kept as a funeral chapel until the early 1920s. Until 1970 occasional special acts of worship had been held at Harvest Festival or on St.Bartholomew's day but in 1980 the church was sold to Hampshire County Council for £5 and incorporated as part of the Manor Farm Country Park.

St. Bartholomew's Church 2005

Photo:- DH Stokes

MANOR FARM

Manor Farm c.1950

Photo:- Hampshire Record Office (65M89/Z29/15)

Half a mile south of Botley's High Street is Manor Farm.

This farm building, also formerly called Botley Farm, has a history dating back well over 500 years. The farmhouse, the earliest part of which dates from medieval times, still shows the blackened roof timbers, evidence of the domestic fires used for heating and cooking in the original fifteenth-century open hall.

Over the centuries the farmhouse has undergone extensive development as successive owners improved the accommodation in line with their needs and their available wealth.

The farm was occupied by tenant farmers who farmed it on behalf of the Lord of the Manor. The agricultural land area of the Farm in 1735 amounted to 278 acres (112 hectares) plus woodland.[12]

In 1979 Hampshire County Council created the Manor Farm Country Park of 400 acres (162 hectares) and in 1984 converted the Farmhouse into a working farm museum.

Led by Arthur Tickner and Gordon Freeman, a few enthusiastic villagers undertook the clearance of the ancient village pond near Manor Farm in 1972. It was this event that led to the formation of the *Botley & Curdridge Local History Society* later that year.

12. HRO 5M53/1493

BOTLEY MILLS

Botley Mills c.1955.

Photo:- Hampshire Record Office (93M94/14/6)

A mill has existed in Botley before the Norman invasion. The Domesday Survey of 1086 for Botley includes '.....*Here is a church and four servants and two mills let at 20 shillings...*' There has been some speculation about two mills. This may have been a reference to another mill further upstream from the known site at Mill Hill but records show that in 1536, a Thomas Everard rented the mill consisting of *'two mills under one roof with stream for £15 a year'*. This description probably meant two water wheels each driving one pair of mill stones and hence the site has always been referred to as Botley *Mills* and not Mill.

The known ownership of the Mills commenced with a Saxon named Cheping. After the Norman occupation the Manor of Botley with its Mills was owned by Ralph de Mortimer and the Mills remained in the possession of the Lords of the Manor until it was sold by James Warner in 1838.

During the period of ownership by the Lords of the Manor, the Mills were let and records exist of the tenants and the rentals paid from 1536 until 1838. One such tenant was Robert Stares, an evil and detested man who became known as 'King Stares'. It was during Stares' tenancy in 1770 that the Mills were enlarged and the main central building we see today is the result of this expansion. Robert Stares died in 1798

In 1838 the site was bought by W & J Clarke and the Mills traded under that name until 1921. For a short time between 1830 and 1848 paper was also manufactured on this site. As well as grinding and trading cereals the Company also traded in coal, importing it in barges.

BOTLEY MILLS

In 1921 the Botley Flour Milling Company Limited was formed and in 1928 it was sold to the Appleby family.

The Appleby family have been involved in milling since the early eighteenth century, when the firm of Joseph Appleby & Sons Ltd. built and acquired mills in the north of England. They moved to the South to acquire the Botley Flour Milling Company and ownership has remained with the Appleby family ever since.

years, the processing of flour and animal feeds was transferred to a new site at Hedge End. From here the mill supplied specialist feeds to many countries in the European Union.

Commercial white flour production continued at Botley until 1990 and stone ground flour until 1993 when, for economic reasons, production ceased.

The historic Botley site now incorporates a

Aerial picture of Botley Mills viewed from the north. c.1925

Photo:Hampshire Record Office (93M94/14/1)

In the latter half of the twentieth century the Applebys diversified by including the manufacture and supply of animal feed in addition to their main business.

A devastating fire in 1980 destroyed the four storey nineteenth-century animal feed plant at Botley and, during the following few

parade of small shops and it is hoped that in the future the Mill itself will be transformed into a working Mill Museum .

BOTLEY MILLS

The Hatches above the millstream. c.1920

Photo:- Arthur Kilford Collection (HRO 59A01/69)

An early Mill delivery vehicle with Tom Kimber (right) and his son Arthur

Photo:- By kind permission of the Appleby family

PRIMARY SCHOOL

Botley Primary School. The picture was taken shortly after the south extension was added in 1899

Photo:- Arthur Kilford Collection (HRO 59A01/105)

Education in Botley was first recorded in 1830 when the Rev Blackburn, Minister of the Chapel in Winchester Street, ran a boys' boarding school from a house in Winchester Street. In 1841 Thomas Baker, son of the Rector Richard Baker, was a tutor of a small boarding school for boys at the Old Rectory in Brook Lane. A small Ladies' School was run by a Miriam Hollis in the 1840s also in Winchester Street.

All these schools were fee paying and only the children of the affluent of the village attended.

In 1855, the Rector, Canon John Morley Lee was instrumental in building the village school on land provided by James Warner of Steeple Court. With donations from prominent members of the village each subscribing £25 and a donation from the National Society, a Church Institution, the school was built at a total cost of £700. It opened on 1st January 1856, to a design by

PRIMARY SCHOOL

John Colson. The building comprised one large classroom that could be divided in two by a folding screen. The Headmaster's house adjoined the building on its eastern side.

The school was known as the National School and was administered by the Rector, churchwardens and elected members of the community.

This was 14 years before the 1870 Education Act which introduced partially funded board schools to provide primary education throughout the country. The Act also supported church schools to operate in parallel with state schools and also provided state funding for employing staff and maintenance of church school buildings. This funding helped to enlarge the school in 1876 by building a new classroom on its northern side (the left hand side of our photograph). It was further enlarged by extending the original school building on the south side in 1899.

The salary of the Head Teacher in 1897 was £119-2s-9d (£119.14p) per annum and the Needlework teacher received £17 p.a .

Schools in the nineteenth and twentieth century were sometimes affected by particular local circumstances. For example, at Botley in June 1899 it was announced *'It is intended to have the summer holidays this year during the strawberry season instead of August as heretofor'*.

During the Second World War air raid shelters were built in the school grounds for the use of the children and staff but the *Hampshire Chronicle* of 20th July 1940 reported *'that the air raid shelters in the school playground will be available for the use of the general public except during school hours and for an hour before the time of opening'*

One local resident recalls that children from Gosport were evacuated to Botley in the early years of the war and, to accommodate them at school, Botley children attended in the mornings and the evacuees in the afternoon. This was just as well because it was known that both groups of children didn't get on with each other.

The Education Act of 1944 created two types of church schools:

Voluntary Aided in which the school was owned by Trustees as part of a church educational trust, the church governors being in the majority. The governing body employed the staff; were responsible for the maintenance of the building and for funding improvements. Religious Education was taught in accordance with the provision of the Trust Deed.

Voluntary Controlled in which the school was owned by Trustees as part of the church educational trust, with the church governors being in the minority. The Local Education Authority employed staff and were responsible for the maintenance of the buildings and for admissions to the school. Religious Education was taught in accordance with the locally agreed syllabus.

PRIMARY SCHOOL

Botley School opted for voluntary control status and hence the school today is known as Botley Church of England (controlled) Primary School.

As pupil numbers rose, it became necessary to increase the accommodation and, in the late 1960s, a new school building was constructed.

The school's Parent Teacher Association built the school's swimming pool in conjunction with the Local Education Authority in 1971.

In the new millennium the original 1855 building became redundant and the old Victorian school buildings were sold and converted into 3 residential cottages in 2000.

Botley School Group 1 Infants Class 1899

Photo:- Botley & Curdridge LHS (PH144)

RECREATION GROUND

By a deed dated 31st January 1887[13], Henry Jenkyns of Botley Hill House conveyed 3.9 acres of land to the south side of the High street to the Ecclesiastical Parish of Botley. Its use was to provide a Recreation Ground for villagers and was to comprised £320 for the land of which £60 was a donation by Henry Jenkyns for fencing, gates, turf and labour. Donors included local residents with the Rector, the Rev Canon Lee (£50) and Mrs Lee (£50) being the principal contributors.

Celebrating Coronation Day c.1911 at Botley Recreation Ground

Photo:- Arthur Kilford Collection (HRO 59A01/90)

be held by James Clark, a miller and Alfred Pern, surgeon, Churchwardens of the parish. The ground was to be managed subject to the trusts and conditions declared in the deed.

The cost of the ground was £331 which

The ground was officially opened by Mrs Lee on 21st June 1888 and designated as the Jubilee Recreation Ground to celebrate the occasion of fifty years of the reign of Queen Victoria. The opening was followed by a cricket match between teams

RECREATION GROUND

representing the married and single men of the village. In the same year village football and cricket teams were formed and in 1891 it is reported that a football match between the Butchers of Hampshire and the Butchers of Portsmouth was played.

A thatched pavilion was built by Messrs W Bailey in June 1890 at a cost of £68 by the generosity of the Rector.

Following the passing of the Parish Councils' Act in 1894, the management and administration of the Recreation Ground was transferred from the Vestry of Botley to Botley Parish Council on 27th September 1898.[14]

The Ground has staged many parades; to celebrate the ending of two world wars; 'Coronations'; national anniversaries; carnivals; concerts and regular sporting contests, in addition to providing an entertainment park for children.

In 1973, following a Public Enquiry, land adjacent to the west of the Recreation Ground was compulsorily purchased by the County Council to extend the public recreation area by another 3.64 acres. The ground had been previously purchased in 1968 by the Brook House Country Club (Hampshire) Ltd., when the Ministry of Housing & Local Government had already approved its allocation for public open space

purposes in 1966. Purchase of the site by agreement had not been possible despite considerable negotiation.

To this extension the Council added the Botley Centre in 1982. A Scout Headquarters was constructed by the parents and friends of the Broad Oak Scout Troop and a young children's play area constructed, financed largely from a collection for a memorial to Alfred Pern, the much loved and respected former local doctor.

In 1978, a part of the land known as Carter's Orchard was given to the Parish Council by Hampshire County Council and added to the south side of the original recreation area.

The original play area for children was completely replaced in 2002. The old Scout Hut headquarters was removed to make way for a purpose built building to accommodate youth activities to include scouts, guides, youth club and an after school club.

A Multi Use Games Area was introduced to the Recreation Ground in the Summer of 2006 to provide a floodlit sports training facility.

14. HRO99A02/F1

FIRE SERVICE

Fire Station on the north side of the High Street. Built in 1940 it was manned by the full time Fire Service until 1945 when it was staffed by the Botley Volunteer Fire Brigade. It was decommissioned in 1973, when the new station was built in Winchester Street, and converted into a house. The building was demolished in 2004.

Photo:- By kind permission of Ralph Deacon

The proposal to form a Fire Brigade was discussed at a Parish Meeting in 1898 and again in 1902 but was rejected on both occasions. It was argued that the initial expense and maintenance costs would be too much for the village to bear.

A series of inexplicable fires occurred in the area in 1913/14 and arson was strongly suspected. Two of these fires were serious enough to call for the assistance from the Southampton Fire Brigade although villagers always rallied around to form a bucket chain from the water supply to the scene of the fire.

It is recorded that in October 1893, when a fire occurred in the back part of Botley Hill House, the residence of Sir Henry Jenkyns, on the alarm being given about 150 helpers of both sexes, rich and poor, rushed to the blaze and formed a line from the house to the river presumably with buckets brought from their homes and kept the flames in check with a good supply of water. Telegrams had been sent to the

FIRE SERVICE

Southampton and Bishop's Waltham Fire Brigades requesting their help and with their combined efforts and that of the villagers the flames were subdued after several hours of hard work.

One of the unexplained fires broke out at Botley Post Office in the evening of 19th January 1914. The alarm was given by the local police constable who was on duty in the Square. He alerted people living in the vicinity by blowing his police whistle. Fear was felt for the Postmistress and her daughters, who were thought to be in the living accommodation over the Post Office. After several unsuccessful attempts by the helpers to reach the upstairs rooms, it was found that the ladies had made their escape and were in a place of safety. After it was discovered that no one was left in the building the volunteers concentrated on dousing the flames. Several climbed through the plate glass window which had been broken by the policeman with his truncheon.

After much effort the flames were extinguished. Had they taken hold they would have destroyed the whole block of buildings down to the corner of the Square, including the Catherine Wheel.

It was now the opinion of public spirited villagers of Botley that it was essential that the village must prepare itself to combat the threat of fires. A group of prominent inhabitants including the Rev. John Jenkyns of Steeple Court, Mr Woodrow of Sarum House, Mr F Bailey, Mr W H Lewry, Mr L Blackman and others, formed themselves into a Fire Appliance Committee whose object was to raise funds for the purpose of buying a fire engine.

This was done by public subscription, generous donations and house to house collections. The committee did their work well for, within a few months, enough money had been raised to purchase a fire engine. A deputation was sent to London to inspect various appliances. They selected a second hand horse drawn 'London Brigade Manual Fire Engine' manufactured by Messrs. Shand and Mason. Supplied with a wide variety of equipment including hoses, a stand pipe, nozzles etc., it could be drawn either by hand or by horse.

The machine arrived at Botley on 8th May 1914 and was put on display outside the Market Hall. A considerable amount of interest was shown as it stood gleaming red with the words 'Botley' emblazoned on both sides in large gold paint.

So the Botley Volunteer Fire Brigade was born. The appliance was housed firstly in the yard of the Catherine Wheel and subsequently in a shed in the yard of Botley Mills for which a rent of 2 shillings (10p) per annum was charged.

The Botley Brigade never owned a horse: the first available animal that happened to be passing by was pressed into service. In the event of a fire, the method of calling out the firemen was by ringing a hand bell, which was kept in a glass fronted case, made by Mr Fred Bailey, affixed to his store shed adjoining the Market Hall.

FIRE SERVICE

Botley's Retained Fire Crew at their new Fire Station in Winchester Street
(Commissioned in 1973)

Back Row L to R: Firemen Maurie Mintrum, Roger West, Bob Biggs, Nigel Lewry, Mick Gibson, Ray Bone, Gordon Biggs & Jack May

Front Row L.to R: Ldg.Fireman Mick Lombard, Sub Officer Pat Parsons, Ldg. Fireman Ralph Deacon, and Ldg. Fireman Jim Elliott.

Photo:- By kind permission of Ralph Deacon

FIRE SERVICE

The very next day after the arrival of the appliance, another mysterious fire broke out, this time in the outbuildings of Sherecroft. Unfortunately the fire engine was not used possibly because the men were not familiar with its workings.

It was arranged for Botley Firemen to receive immediate instruction and a Sgt. Lock of the Portsmouth Fire Brigade was enlisted to help.

When Botley Mills bought their first motor lorry in 1919 (an ex War Department lorry with solid tyres and chain driven to the rear wheels) the shafts were removed from the fire engine and a towing attachment fitted in its place, to enable the engine to be towed behind the motor vehicle.

By 1929 it was decided that a more modern pump was necessary and it was agreed that Mr Roxburgh of Roxburgh and Scivier, Botley Garages, be asked to construct a trailer pump. Roxburgh produced an appliance consisting of a Singer motor car engine coupled to an ex Admiralty pump purchased from Portsmouth Dockyard. The whole was mounted on two wheels and fitted with a towing attachment. The total cost of £70 was raised by public subscription. The pump was tested against a Southampton Fire Brigade pump and deemed to be satisfactory by the Chief of the Southampton Brigade.

The method of raising the money to pay for this new addition to the Brigade was the same as in 1914, by public subscription. The total cost was duly paid to Mr Roxburgh. The Winchester Rural District council donated £2.

A siren was fitted to the roof of Mr Fred Bailey's shop (next to the Market Hall) in 1931 as a means of calling out the volunteer firemen, a more efficient method than the old handbell.

The members of the Brigade were very public spirited and enthusiastic because the financial remuneration was very small. They only received a few shillings for each fire attended if the property was insured against fire. Insurance companies were often unwilling to pay up without considerable negotiation.

With the coming of Air Raid Precautions and the passing of the Fire Brigade Act in 1938, responsibility for the Fire Brigade passed to the Winchester Rural District Council, although the same men continued to serve the Brigade. So ended the Botley Volunteer Fire Brigade after 24 years of service.

Botley's fire station continues to be served by Retained Firemen from the village.

CURDRIDGE HISTORY

The name Curdridge derives from Cuthred's Ridge. The 'Ridge' is probably the high ground to the west of the village above the River Hamble but it is unclear who or what was Cuthred.

Bishop's Waltham and surrounding lands, including Curdridge, were granted to Denewulf, Bishop of Winchester by King Edward the Elder in the year 904[15]. The Bishops held the manor until 1551 when Bishop Poynet conveyed the property to Paulet, the Lord Treasurer (a representative of the Crown), in return for a fixed annual income. Seven years later, Queen Mary restored the manor to John White, Bishop of Winchester and his successors and they continued to hold the manor until the sale of the Bishops' lands in 1647. Bishop's Waltham was then purchased by Robert Reynolds for the sum of £8000. At the Restoration in 1660, the manor was restored to the Bishops of Winchester and they retained their hold upon it until the Bishops' Resignation Act of 1869 when all lands, tithes etc. passed into the hands of the Ecclesiastical Commissioners.

Until 1838, Curdridge remained a tithing of the parish of Bishop's Waltham. On the 1st February 1838 the ecclesiastical parish of Curdridge was formed comprising an area of 2172 acres of land (879 hectares) and in 1894 the Civil Parish of Curdridge was created.

Prior to 1865, a large portion of Curdridge was open common land which allowed the villagers to graze their livestock, collect firing and to grow crops. Curdridge Common extended as a rough triangle from the present junction of the Waltham and Wickham roads, to approximately, the Cricketers' pond and Kitnock's house. Dwellings developed around this area of common land with one part evolving to the north around where the church and school were subsequently built and a southern development extending north east from a point half way along what is now Outlands Lane.

Curbridge became part of Curdridge civil parish in 1950 when Curbridge was divided between Curdridge and Wickham. Curdridge acquired the area around the creek including the Horse and Jockey and St. Barnabas Church. The church is still administered by Sarisbury Green.

15. Victoria History of the Counties of England, Vol..3 pp 276-279

CURDRIDGE HISTORY

Unveiling of the horse trough at the entrance to Botley Station to celebrate the occasion of the Diamond Jubilee of the reign of Queen Victoria. It was funded by the villagers of Curdridge and unveiled on 23rd April 1898 by Curdridge Parish Council. Today, though the column is somewhat shorter, the memorial is still sited at the station entrance alongside the memorial to the murder of Thomas Webb.

Photo:-Botley & Curdridge LHS (PH300)

CURDRIDGE CHURCHES

Until 1838 Curdridge was a tithing and villagers had to travel to Bishop's Waltham to attend their Parish Church.

With the rector of Bishop's Waltham in the chair, a meeting was convened in Curdridge on 11th June 1834, to address the problem of the lack of a church in the parish. It was resolved to press for a Chapel of Ease and that *'the spot of ground near Pound Farm to be fixed upon for the site'* There followed petitions, plans and appeals for funds and by September that year the Rev. John Haygarth, the Rural Dean, had laid the foundation stone.[16] The actual site of this Chapel was just to the north of the present church.

The chapel was designed by Mr G Guillaume of Southampton and built by Thomas Gurman at a cost of £1300. It was a substantial building of brick, rendered with cement. It had a spire, a bell and a gallery for choir and organ and sittings for 333. (The population of Curdridge at that time was 400).

The Chapel was consecrated on 27th August 1835 by the Bishop of Winchester the Right Reverend Charles Sumner.

The first Curate in Charge was Richard Chenevix Trench (1807-1886). Chenevix Trench came to Curdridge in 1835 and made his home in Sherecroft House. He spent six years at the Chapel and it saw the growth of his reputation as a scholar and equally significant the development of his friendship with Samuel Wilberforce, son of William Wilberforce, the anti-slavery campaigner. In 1841, Chenevix Trench was appointed curate to Wilberforce, Rector

at Alverstoke, near Gosport.

Chenevix Trench was later to become Archbishop of Dublin (1856). He died in 1886 and is buried in Westminster Abbey.

Over the next 45 years, the Chapel of Ease gradually became dilapidated and the increasing congregation began to exceed the available seating. There became an urgent need to provide a new church and a site on the Glebe land adjoining the Chapel was selected.

A design by Mr Jackson ARA (later Sir Thomas) was accepted for the church and funding efforts were planned.

Richard Chenevix Trench. (1807-1886)

Botley & Curdridge LHS (PH557)

16. Hogg J. *Curdridge & St.Peter's Church* (1988)

CURDRIDGE CHURCHES

The design of St. Peter's in Curdridge was in the style of fifteenth-century English Gothic. Several features are typical of Jackson's work: the substantial proportions; the polygonal turrets; his handling of the flintwork and the use of small carved stone figures, in this instance eight gargoyles, carved by Farmer & Brindley.

In 1887 Messrs Dobson of Colchester started work on the foundations, fortuitously aided by tons of sand and gravel brought from the clearance of Botley High Street, following the Hamble's great flood which swept into the Mill.

The foundation stone was laid by Miss Augusta Burrell of Fairthorne Manor, a main benefactor of the fund. Although the plans included a Tower, it was omitted from the original construction until sufficient money became available. So during construction of the main building the West arch was closed with brickwork until the tower could be added to that end of the building.

Consecration of the church took place on

Chapel of Ease, Curdridge 1835-1888

Photo:- Botley & Curdridge LHS (PH552)

CURDRIDGE CHURCHES

the 6th November, 1888. The ceremony was conducted by the Lord Bishop of the Diocese, the Right Rev E H Browne, with the Vicar the Rev G W Hills.

Meanwhile, after the distribution of the fitments, including the single bell and small font, the chapel was demolished. The bricks and rubble were taken to the Recreation Ground (in Curdridge) and used to level the cricket pitch.

In 1894, through generous donations in memory of Charles Cory, a previous donor for the building of the church in 1887, the construction of the tower; a clock; a peal of eight bells; a stained glass window for the Chancel and new oak pews all became a reality and were incorporated in the church by the end of that year. The tower was completed in less than seven months.

The Tower The tower is 65 feet to the top parapet and 22 feet square and is divided internally into three floor levels. At ground level the vestibule contains the Font and memorial wall tablets. This room has two corner wall shafts, the north-east corner giving access to the clock weights, sheaves and cables, at ground level. In the south-east corner, a door leads to a spiral stone staircase, within a circular brick shaft, lit by narrow slot windows in the wall of the tower, which gives access to the upper chambers and roof. At the 24 feet Level a door leads to the bell ringing chamber, which also houses the clock and its drives to the three faces. At the 48 feet Level is the bell chamber. A further 15 feet up, the shaft is formed into a small tower with an octagonal roof, a door opening on to the roof of the tower.

St.Peter's Church, Curdridge built in 1887. The tower was not added until 1894

Photo:- Botley & Curdridge LHS (PH279)

CURDRIDGE CHURCHES

Interior The plan comprises the Chancel, with organ and vestry, the Nave and the Tower Vestibule. The design provides for an aisle to be added, if required, to the north side of the Nave.

The church is well lit. All the windows were originally of plain glass. As a result of memorial gifts, seven of them have been replaced in stained glass. The alabaster Reredos by Farmer & Brindley was installed in 1907. Its three panels depict at the centre the seated figure of Christ, with four kneeling angels on each of the two side panels.

Overhead is a flattened barrel type roof with close spaced plain frames. The organ is set in the north wall of the Chancel, projecting through an arch into the vestry. The paving is of black, white and grey marble in geometric pattern. At the foot of the Chancel steps on the north side, stands the pulpit of wainscot oak with linenfold panels and tracery. The pulpit is mounted on a Portland stone base. On the south side is a brass lectern. Oak choir stalls were completed in 1894.

Nave Oak pews were installed at the same time as the choir stalls.

C.1920. Curdridge Church built in 1887. Tower added in 1894

Photo:- Arthur Kilford Collection (HRO 59A01/71)

CURDRIDGE CHURCHES

The roof structure over the Nave has a design involving ten frames, spaced with long collars, each with a king post and supported by wall posts set on stone corbels. Ample, arched braces and longitudinal arched braces give strength to the structure.

Bells The gift of a peal of eight bells in 1894 were cast by John Taylor & Sons of Loughborough. Their total weight was 4¾ tons (4836Kg). They were mounted on steel guides with iron stays.

Churchyard There are four gates to the churchyard, the oldest being the Chapelgate which led to the old Chapel of Ease and to the Bier house. A short distance south is the West gate. The south gate on the Botley Road was made as a Lychgate in 1890. The North gate near the school was rehung in 1984 with one made from the wheel of HMS Amethyst, the frigate which became famous in fighting her way out of the River Yangtse in 1949. The wheel was given by Mrs Birnie in memory of her husband Sandy and their son Alistair. It is

Interior of St.Peter's Church, Curdridge

Photo:- Arthur Kilford Collection (HRO 59A01/142)

CURDRIDGE CHURCHES

sad to record that the 'wheel' was stolen in 2004 and has been replaced by a replica.

The war memorial cross was erected in 1920.

Vicarage The first vicarage was built on the corner of Botley Road and, what is now known as, Vicarage Lane (the building is now known as Beechcroft). The present vicarage was built on Glebe land by the former chapel in 1883.

RECREATION GROUND AND READING ROOM

Curdridge Common was enclosed in 1856. Four acres of the common was allotted to the Church Wardens and Overseers of the Poor of Bishop's Waltham as a place for exercise and recreation for the villagers. This area is known as 'The Plantation' and is opposite the Cricketers Pond on the Bishop's Waltham road.

In 1884, five acres of land in the centre of Curdridge was purchased from Mr John Gater of West End at a net cost of £945. This was met by Sir Henry Jenkyns of Botley Hill House and Robert Burrell and his sister Augusta of Fairthorne Manor. The purchase was made on the understanding that the Ground should be placed under the control of the inhabitants of Curdridge. This was

View of St. Peter's Church and the Reading Room looking north east. c.1900

Photo:-Botley & Curdridge LHS (PH131)

The ground was used for cricket by Bishop's Waltham as early as 1838 in a fixture against Titchfield. Following the Act of Enclosure, Curdridge formed their own Cricket Club.

It was considered that the Plantation was not particularly suited to cricket due to its size, shape and condition of the soil.

approved by the Charity Commissioners under a scheme whereby the ground would be administered by eight elected members appointed by the Vestry of Curdridge.

After the introduction of the 1894 Local Government Act, the nomination of Managers was made by Curdridge Parish Council and in 1950 they were augmented

RECREATION GROUND AND READING ROOM

Government Act, the nomination of Managers was made by Curdridge Parish Council and in 1950 they were augmented by representatives from village organisations.[17]

The Recreation Ground was improved in 1946 by the introduction of a children's corner, football pitch and a partial levelling of the ground.

was considered to be impractical. Improvements were limited to levelling the ground at the entrance and to providing a hard standing car park and a lawn and gravelled path laid adjacent to the Reading Room.

Three quarters of an acre of the land acquired in 1884 was used to provide a

Curdridge Show, 1964, looking north across the Recreation Ground. The housing at St. Peter's Close is seen under construction.

Photo:- Botley & Curdridge LHS (PH290)

the ground.

An investigation was undertaken in 1958 to see what improvements could be made to level the whole of the ground. It was estimated that it would require the excavation of 18000 cu.yds (13122 cu.mtrs.) of soil, banking and resowing to provide a level football ground and would cost between £8000 and £10000 at that time. It

Reading Room and cottage (for the use of a caretaker). A small Reading Room had already been provided at the original vicarage.

Again the cost of the building was met largely by the generosity of Sir Henry Jenkyns and the Burrells. It was administered by four trustees.

17. HRO 35M84/174

RECREATION GROUND AND READING ROOM

The Reading Room was enlarged by the generosity of Augusta Burrell with the addition of two small rooms in 1896 and, in 1923, the billiard room was added, the main hall enlarged and an acetylene gas plant was installed to provide lighting in place of oil lamps. The cost of these improvements were met by Miss Burrell herself, Lady Jenkyns, Miss E Jenkyns and the Curdridge Women's Institute.

In 1948 the Charity Commissioners approved a Trust Deed by which the Reading Room was to be administered by a Management Committee consisting of the Vicar, a representative from each of the village organisations, four representatives elected at the Annual Parish Meeting, and since 1957, three parish councillors were also appointed.

It was found that the letting charges were inadequate to finance the maintenance of the Reading Room and it was impractical to increase the charges which would have prevented many organisations from using the Hall. To meet these costs, an Entertainment Committee was formed and in 1956 they introduced the annual Curdridge Show. This has proved to be a very successful event in southern Hampshire's diary and makes a very significant contribution towards the upkeep of the Reading Room.

Reading Room looking north. c.1970

Photo:- Botley & Curdridge LHS (PH251)

PRIMARY SCHOOL

Curdridge Primary School 1913

Photo:- Botley & Curdridge LHS (PH264)

Following the building of the Chapel of Ease in 1835, the villagers sought to provide a school for children. The then new Curate at the Chapel, Richard Chevenix Trench led the campaign for a school. Applications for financial assistance were made to the *National Society for Promoting the Education of the Poor in the Principles of the Established Church* and the Treasury in 1837. The Bishop of Winchester granted a plot of land of one rod adjacent to the church and the estimated cost of the single classroom school building was £120. The local gentry provided £68 and a National grant of £30 was received. The building was built of brick under a slate roof but very modest in size being 8ft. by 15ft. The school room was completed in 1839 and one paid teacher, Miss Maria Short, was employed at £5 per annum.

The school was totally inadequate for the number of children in Curdridge and in 1865 land was acquired next to the school room to increase its size.

The existing school building was expanded and School Managers appointed. The first resolution of the Managers was to provide a lump sum pension to the present school mistress, Miss Short, for her 25 years of service and, with donations from villagers, a sum of £18-13s-0d (£18.65p) was paid to her. Fees were agreed at 2d, 5d, and 9d according to the ability of the parents to pay. Third and fourth children from the same family were to be charged at half price.[18]

Miss Sarah Jane Field was appointed as

18.HRO 98M82

PRIMARY SCHOOL

Mistress at a salary of £30 per annum plus £10 for lodgings. She resigned three years later.

The Reverend Hills was appointed Vicar in 1867 and replaced the former incumbent, Henry Howell, as chairman of the School Managers. He sought permission to use the school rooms in the evenings as a reading room, to conduct bible classes or to give secular lectures. The managers refused on the grounds that the conditions of the grant for the school defined by the Bishop permitted only the teaching of children. Later in 1878, he took his request to the Bishop's Waltham School Board, overseers of the Curdridge School Managers, but with no more success.

The senior mistress in 1870 complained to the Managers that many children were only bringing 1d per week for fees. The Managers instructed her to send children home if proper payments were not met.

It wasn't until the 1891 Elementary Education Act that schools were enabled to cease charging for elementary education.

Major works to the school were undertaken in 1872 when the school yard was levelled, fences heightened and new closets were constructed.

With increasing numbers of children attending the school it became necessary to introduce a new temporary classroom in the 1970s. Further expansion was required later when another temporary classroom was added.

In 2007 a major building programme expanded the school and replaced the temporary classrooms. The school can accommodate up to 120 children.

FAIRTHORNE MANOR

Fairthorne Manor, Curdridge. c.1970

Fairthorne Manor stands on the east bank of the River Hamble and today is the home of the YMCA.

The Manor was built in 1854 and is a good example of Victorian architecture. It was built as a country residence for Clement Milward QC, treasurer of the Middle Temple in London and a man of some standing.[19]

In 1878 a large part of the estate was sold for £52000 to Robert Anthony Burrell and his sister Augusta. The Burrells were from a family of wealthy mine owners in Durham.

The estate at this time comprised the manor house and 120 acres and was increased when Augusta bought the adjoining estate from the Reverend Jenkyns, adding a further 80 acres.

Under the Burrells' management, the Fairthorne Estate underwent a period o prosperity and development. They enlargec the manor house and planted the magnificent chestnut avenue alongside the present golf course providing a short cut to the station and Botley village.

When it became necessary to replace the Chapel of Ease with a new church, the Burrells donated £1500 of the necessary £6000. Augusta Burrell laid the foundatior stone for the new church on November 29th 1887. The brass lectern in the church is inscribed *'Given by Augusta Burrell o Fairthorne Manor Ann. Dom MDCCCLXXXVIII'*.

19.Jones June *Fairthorne-Past & Present (ISBN 0951057014)*

FAIRTHORNE MANOR

In 1902, Kitnocks House in Curdridge was severely damaged by fire and it was rebuilt from funds provided by Miss Burrell and when complete the house was given as a wedding present to her god-daughter Edith Randolph.

Robert Burrell died in June 1910 aged 81 and as a memorial to her brother, Augusta had a stained glass window incorporated in Curdridge Church and endowed the Accident wing of the Royal South Hants. Hospital in Southampton.

Augusta remained at Fairthorne and continued to be generous to both Botley and Curdridge. After the First World War, she made up the necessary total for the Curdridge War Memorial Fund and gave many gifts to St. Peter's and All Saints churches. She set up trust funds for the needy and to provide a nurse for the villages. She also gave numerous donations to Southampton and Winchester Hospitals and to the hospital of her old home of Durham.

Augusta died on 25th April 1924 and was buried beside her brother in Curdridge churchyard.

Fairthorne Manor was left to her god-daughter, Edith Randolph but she died a month before Augusta and thus the Manor became the property of Edith's husband, Major Randolph.

In 1925 Randolph sold the property to Dame Mary Rose Barrington the wife of Sir Charles Burton Barrington, but retained the land adjacent to the Manor extending south to Eyersdown Copse.

Sir Charles Barrington had been educated at Rugby and Trinity College, Dublin and was a very keen sportsman. Shortly before he died at the age of 95 he gave the trustees of the Curdridge Reading Room a silver shield which had been presented to him by Irish tenants in 1876 to commemorate the winning of the Philadelphia Graduate Cup for rowing; it was said at that time it was the only challenge cup to have been brought out of the USA by a rowing team. The shield is in high relief and was designed by the French artist Gustave Doré. It represents Milton's Paradise Lost. The shield is displayed in the Reading Room.

At the outbreak of World War 2, the army moved into the house in 1940 but the Barringtons stayed on until they both died in 1943. Both are buried in Botley churchyard.

CURDRIDGE STREET SCENES

Curdridge Lane looking east. c.1920

Photo:-Botley & Curdridge LHS (PH254)

Gordon Road looking east. c.1920

Photo:-Botley & Curdridge LHS (PH262)

CURDRIDGE STREET SCENES

Horse and Jockey Public House, Curbridge. 1903

Photo:-Botley & Curdridge LHS (PH249)

Cricketers Pond c.1920

Photo:- Botley & Curdridge LHS (PH261)

CURDRIDGE STREET SCENES

The Mount, Calcot Lane. c.1905

Photo:-Botley & Curdridge LHS (PH257)

Curdridge Upper Post Office. c.1920

Photo Arthur Kilford Collection (HRO 59A01/70)

THE RIVER HAMBLE

The River Hamble at Botley showing the boathouse. c.1920. Now the site of Hamblewood and Hambleside
Photo:- By kind permission of Brian Powell

The River Hamble extends for 11½ miles from Bishop's Waltham to Southampton Water and provides Botley with 6½ miles of parish boundary on its eastern and southern sides.

Almost certainly both the siting of the old village (at Manor Farm) and the present village were influenced by the presence of the river. Mesolithic finds have been made on the west bank of the river here, and there is significant evidence of the Roman occupation at this point.[20] The Roman road that runs just south of the Manor Farm buildings crossed the river close to the present-day sewage works, and archaeologists have excavated a stone

causeway. There is also the associated villa site just below Fairthorne Manor. Later in the medieval period, the crossing moved to a less hazardous part of the river—water levels had risen by then—and it is likely that this caused the village to migrate northwards to its present position.

The river provided power to drive the mills for paper and corn and has been used for centuries as a transport route.

Before the turnpike road improvements of the eighteenth century, the river would have been the preferred method of carrying goods

THE RIVER HAMBLE

and people between the many ports and wharves of the Solent. Corn, coal and stone were transported up river to the Mill or the Quay and flour, timber and underwood were sent downstream. Small barges were used with the tides to and from Botley to rendezvous with cargo vessels moored at Bursledon.

The Quay at Botley became an industrial centre and housed many stores, wharves, coal yards and boathouses. By the middle of the eighteenth century it had become 'a free wharf for all the copyhold tenants of Botley'. In 1839 the tithe map shows that there were substantial timber yards as well as a bark store and a shed where mast hoops were steamed and bent. The

residential housing of Hamblewood Court and Quayside have been built over much of this site and only a small part of this historic area now exists. However, what remains provides us with public access to this delightful part of the river. Today the Quay is owned by Hampshire County Council and administered by Botley Parish Council.

The river between the M27 motorway bridge and Botley Quay remains undeveloped and is a beautiful and tranquil landscape that is unique in Hampshire. The only building on this stretch of the river was Pink Mead. This pretty cottage was unfortunately destroyed by fire in 2001. The cottage had

Barge transporting coal to Botley from Bursledon c.1914. The picture shows Augustus Mears of Swanwick at the stern with his son in one of the last journeys undertaken using this mode of transport.

Photo — Botley & Curdridge LHS (PH079)

THE RIVER HAMBLE

served as a public house to provide bargemen and other river users with refreshments. It was known as the Blue Anchor Public House.

In 1927, Major Randolph, put up for sale by auction 70 acres of his land south of Fairthorne to Eyersdown copse near Burridge including the River Cur. The notice of sale included *'twelve attractive building sites'*. The sale announcement caused dismay to many local people and a public meeting at the *Dolphin* in Botley resolved to safeguard the river from building development for all time. A public subscription was initiated with the aim of buying the land and giving it to the National Trust for protection. Mr Hugh Jenkyns of Steeplecourt was the first to bring the public's attention to this sale and he started the subscription by giving £1000 for the purchase of part of the land as a memorial for his daughter Priscilla who had died earlier that year from pneumonia. Another £1200, including £100 from Major Randolph himself, was raised locally and, in 1928, 70 acres along the eastern stretch of the Hamble River was acquired by the National Trust.

Pink Mead Cottage c.1920—Formerly The Blue Anchor Public House

Photo:- Arthur Kilford Collection (HRO 59A01/33)

THE RIVER HAMBLE

Hugh Jenkyns arranged with other landowners along the river to covenant their land to preserve the riverside land. We and future generations will be forever grateful to the public spirit of local people in preserving this beautiful river, and access to it.

Barkstore and Parish Quay c.1920

Photo — Botley & Curdridge LHS (PH072)

THE RAILWAY

London & Southampton Railway locomotive crossing the River Hamble north of Botley Station c.1910.

Photo—Arthur Kilford Collection (HRO 59A01/67)

The London and Southampton Railway Company received Royal Assent for its Bill through Parliament to construct a railway between the Capital and Southampton via Bishopstoke (now Eastleigh) on 25th July 1834. The London terminus was at Nine Elms, Vauxhall, near present day Waterloo and construction commenced in October 1834 and was completed on the 11th May 1840.

In June 1839 an Act of Parliament was granted for a branch line from Bishopstoke to Gosport, thus opening up traffic to Portsmouth and the Isle of Wight. Construction of the branch line commenced in 1839 and the census return for Botley in 1841, which was taken six months before the opening of the line, showed that 40 men, listed as 'Excavators', resided in the Winchester Street and Boorley Green areas of Botley and presumably worked on the new railway.

THE RAILWAY

Railcar, introduced in 1904 on the Botley/Bishop's Waltham branchline. The Railcar or Railmotor was a locomotive and carriage combined on a single underframe which could accommodate 28 first class and 32 third class passengers.

Photo—Arthur Kilford Collection (HRO 59A01/85)

The site chosen for Botley station was in a cutting ½ mile from the village centre in the Parish of Curdridge and cost £1250. The first passenger train ran on 29th November 1841 but four days later the line was closed due to landslips north of Fareham. The line was re-opened on 7th February 1842. The problems of land instability were to manifest themselves again in later years as many slips occurred in the cutting approaching the station - the most notable in January 1936 near Outlands Lane. There have been several subsidences since including one as recently as the winter of 2014, closing the line for 6 weeks.

The timetable for 1842 shows that the cost of single travel to London (Nine Elms) from Botley was 20s-6d (£1.025) first class or 14s-0d (70p) second class. The journey time was 3 hours and 36 minutes. The timetable notes that *'The first class trains convey first class passengers only, excepting that accommodation is afforded for a limited number of servants in livery'.*

THE RAILWAY

On lst June 1863 a new 3½ mile branch line was constructed from Botley station to Bishop's Waltham to serve the new clay works there. Journey time was eight minutes and six trains travelled in each direction on weekdays and three on Sundays.

A Halt was provided near Durley Mill in 1909 at a cost of £44.

Traffic on the new line very quickly increased particularly the conveyance of coal, timber, farm and flourmill products but by the late 1880s the number of improved roads brought about the demise of the Bishop's Waltham branch line and it closed to passenger traffic in 1933 and to freight traffic in 1962.

Station Road looking towards Botley with the Railway Inn on the left hand side. c.1920

Photo: Hampshire Record Office (63A04/B1/3/45)

PEOPLE - William Cobbett

otley is the most delightful village in the world. It has everything, in a village, that I love, and none of the things I hate. It is in a valley; the soil is rich, thickset with wood; the farms are small, the cottages neat; it has neither workhouse nor barber nor attorney nor justice of the peace, and, though last not least, it has no volunteers. There is no justice within six miles of us, and the barber comes three miles once a week to shave and cut hair! "Would I were poetical," I would write a poem in praise of Botley'. So wrote William Cobbett in a letter to John Wright (Editorial assistant of Cobbett's *Political Register*) in 1805.

William Cobbett was born in 1763 at Farnham, Surrey, the son of a farmer. A soldier, farmer, journalist and finally a Member of Parliament, he became the foremost political journalist of his time. A Tory by instinct, Cobbett nevertheless became known as 'The Father of Reform', one of the founders of British Radicalism. Undeterred by fines and imprisonment he continually campaigned for justice for the rural poor and for the reform of Parliament and was finally rewarded in 1832 by the passing of the Reform Act. He died in 1835. Today Cobbett is best remembered for many publications including *Cottage Economy*, *Rural Rides* and his weekly paper *Political Register*.

Cobbett and his family came to Botley in 1805 and purchased Botley House on the west bank of the Hamble River opposite Botley Mills. Robert Stares of Sherecroft, a tenant of Botley Mills, had built the house some ten years earlier. The house was described as *'an ill constructed house at*

William Cobbett 1763—1835

Photo:- Botley & Curdridge LHS (PH347)

Botley which from the number of windows contained in it aptly obtained the name the Lantern House, resembling a church rather than a house and having a large clock in the centre in the shape of a dome.'

During his first three years in Botley, Cobbett undertook the acquisition of many local farms and woodlands in Curdridge and Droxford. These amounted to 643 acres (260 hectares) and cost him more than

PEOPLE - William Cobbett

£27000. Despite income from the sale of timber from these landholdings and £1000 per annum from his weekly *Political Register*, Cobbett was continually in debt, which was to lead him eventually to bankruptcy in 1820.

Cobbett pursued many sports, particularly shooting and fishing and in 1805 he organised a series of Singlestick matches in Botley in which a 1st prize of 15 guineas and a gold laced hat were awarded. Singlestick was played between two contestants who wielded a stick at each other. (The winner was decided by who inflicted a broken head that drew blood from his opponent.)

Richard Baker was the Rector of Botley and he and Cobbett were close friends sharing a common interest in farming and hare coursing. However this harmony did not last. Cobbett found Baker to be as opinionated and as quarrelsome as himself and their politics were diametrically opposed. The villagers of Botley liked Cobbett well enough to give him a rousing welcome on his return from his Newgate imprisonment in 1812 but the Rector refused to allow the church bells to be rung in his honour.

On leaving prison, Cobbett could no longer afford to live at Botley House and he rented Sherecroft Farm. He and his family remained there until 1817 when, fearing a further period in prison, he was forced to flee to America. He returned to Botley briefly at Christmas in 1819 on his return from America, staying at Botley House by the permission of John Tunno, the mortgagee, who had taken possession.

Botley House was purchased by Mr John Jenkyns, a lawyer who owned Botley Hill. The house was by then almost buried by the locust trees planted by Cobbett. Later, Jenkyns demolished it in the 1830s

The Institute of Journalists erected a memorial to Cobbett in 1957 on Mill Hill by the bridge (near to Cobbett's House). The memorial was relocated to the Square in the 1980s.

Cobbett's Botley House stable (right) viewed from Church Lane. Now a private dwelling.

Photo:- Botley & Curdridge LHS (PH028)

PEOPLE - Robert Stares

Robert Stares was one of the most controversial characters to live in Botley and Curdridge. He rented Botley Mills in the eighteenth century, built the house that was subsequently owned by William Cobbett and owned up to 500 acres of land including many farms. But he was unloved by most people of the village because he was alleged to be arrogant, a cheat and a liar.

He was born at Curbridge in the parish of Bishop's Waltham in August 1729, the son of a farmer who rented Fairthorn Farm from the Duke of Portland, Lord of the Manor of Botley.

Stares had a basic education which an early biographer described as *'having an understanding and a judgement which, had they been improved by a suitable education might have placed him in a more exalted situation in society than he held. But as subsequent history develops many transactions void of the first principles which should influence mankind in their actions, it is perhaps not to be regretted that his parents kept him at the level of a common reading and writing school; though possibly the same education which would have improved his talents and increases his knowledge might also have enlarged his mind and ameliorated his heart'.*

When Robert was 15 his family moved to Botley Hill Farm, which was on the site of the present Sherecroft House where he assisted his father in general farm labouring activities.

A friend of the family was a Mr Horner who owned farms and land at Curdridge, Corhampton and Bishop's Waltham and was in business as a mercer, grocer and chandler. He was an old man and had in his care a Miss Williams the daughter of a clergyman. Young Stares was a constant visitor to Horner's properties helping him to manage the farms and buying and selling his stock. Also he was clearly taken by the charms of Miss Williams for they were very soon married.

In 1757 Stares' father died and Harfield Farm and Home Farm both in Curdridge and comprising about 270 acres passed to Robert along with his father's personal possessions.

A few years later Mr Horner died and his will devised to Robert the greater part of his property, which included Mortimer's Farm at Bishopstoke and Roke Farm at Bishop's Waltham. Many persons who claimed to be heirs of the deceased contested Horner's bequests to Stares. One such claim was upheld, where a copyhold estate descended to a Mrs Ann Bristow of Hambledon a lady of 93 years of age, infirm and nearly blind. Robert Stares was dismayed to see this reduction in his growing fortune and persuaded the poor woman to sign away her inheritance to his benefit. It was not known if she received compensation or even knew what she was signing.

Stares was now a rich man and contempories described him as a man of arrogance who was held in high esteem by the poor, who were taken in by his "*fascinating mask of blunt integrity*" and by the less discerning of his social equals which only served to inflate his vanity and self importance. He would not suffer opposition to his views and browbeat those who dared to stand up to him. Such was his notoriety that he became known as 'King Stares'.

Shortly after his father's death, Robert Stares entered the business of miller and became tenant of Botley Mills, owned by the Duke of Portland, and in 1774 purchased New House Farm with land extending to the mill premises.

He acquired Uplands Farm next to New House by dubious means. Uplands was owned by Henry Fielder who also kept the Dolphin Inn at Botley. Fielder had purchased Uplands for £1300 in 1779 and subsequently spent money improving the farm. In 1784 he had some accidental losses and found himself owing money. He was a kind and honest man and anxious to pay off his creditors. He sought the advice of Stares as a friend. Stares recommended to Fielder that he should give up his business and leave the farm to trustees who would settle his debts and provide a living for him. Stares and two others were appointed trustees of the estate and Stares alone undertook to dispose of the property. The other trustees and the creditors had absolute confidence in Stares and allowed him to be the sole acting trustee. Stares set about to sell Fielder's household goods, horses and farming stock and put Uplands Farm up for auction.

The auction was a mockery and showed the arrogance and contempt Stares had for society and the timidity of the community in standing up to this tyrannical and unpleasant man. Many people attended the auction and when the sale started for Uplands Farm, Stares joined the bidding and, such had his reputation become, that other bidders withdrew except a man named Davies who lived in Botley. Stares with much abusive language demanded of Davies why he was bidding and where was he getting his money to pay for it. Stares took him by the shoulders and forcibly removed from the saleroom. The man appalled at the treatment he had received and dreading Stares' resentment left the sale shaken and embarrassed. The auctioneer and people present were silent spectators. Stares became the sole bidder and the estate was knocked down to him for £840. He did not account for the purchase to Mr Fielder's creditors and delayed paying any dividend at all. Henry Fielder was forced to provide for himself and his family by serving as an ostler at the Coach and Horses Inn at Southampton.

Stares continued to purchase property and at one stage owned about 500 acres around his property in Botley. He ring fenced his land holding, rebuilt the barns and outhouses of his several farms, laid out and enclosed the ground around his house (Sherecroft) with high walls. Considerable money was spent rebuilding parts of the mill and adding storehouses and raising the

PEOPLE - Robert Stares

banks of the mill river. He also had constructed a large house for his daughter and son-in-law on the west bank of the Hamble River opposite the mill, a house that was subsequently owned by William Cobbett. This enormous expenditure of money far exceeded the profits from his businesses and he found it necessary to mortgage many of his estates, unknown to his associates. This was eventually to bring about the downfall of Robert Stares.

In the meantime he continued to court the gentry of the County and ride roughshod over those who opposed his views or objectives. Stares was keen to support the Tories, Heathcote and Chute in their quest for election to represent the County in Parliament. He gathered support for the candidates, gave his time, provided public dinners and with great pomp and procession appeared at election meetings. The politicians' Whig opponents were Lord John Russell and Mr Jervoise and when they came to Bishop's Waltham to rally support they stayed at the Crown Inn. The landlord, Mr Perry and his wife could not refuse accommodation to any guests whilst they had room for them. However, Stares was so enraged against the landlord for allowing the opposing politicians accommodation that he took his custom to the White Hart Inn and his associates, millers and farmers followed him. It was the ruin of Perry the landlord, who soon after, was obliged to leave the Crown.

Another incident showing Stares' unsavoury character occurred on Waltham Chase one evening. Stares and two relations had been in Bishop's Waltham and an argument ensued between one of Stares' relations and a Mr Lys a County magistrate. On returning to Botley across the Chase, Mr Lys overtook Stares and his companions. Stares thrust a large stick across Mr Lys horse and shouted *'you damned rascal how dare you make use of my name, I have a great mind to knock you off your horse'.*

Robert Stares had this house built for his daughter in c.1790. It is viewed looking south west from Botley Mills. (From an engraving of 1817)

Photo:- Hampshire Record Office (TOP37/2/2)

PEOPLE - Robert Stares

Lys rode on but Stares' companions rode after him and attacked him with their sticks and whips. Stares encouraged them shouting *'damn him knock him off his horse'*. He was finally assaulted and horse whipped by them all. The three were subsequently prosecuted at the Assizes by Mr Justice Buller. The judge recommended to the parties to compromise the case. The defendants accordingly pleaded guilty and were fined one shilling each.

Due to his vanity Stares fell further into debt. Revelling in the other farmers' admiration of his stock, he delighted in feeding his pigs, oxen and sheep to excess before sending them to market. It was said that he fattened his lambs at vast expense cramming them with oatmeal balls having an infusion of Holland's gin. He failed to achieve a market price in excess of the cost of feed.

As previously stated, it became necessary for Stares to mortgage most of his property to finance his excessive expenditure. He also started borrowing money from friends and such was his apparent standing that he did not promptly repay these loans. Finally in 1793 he put before his creditors a statement of his financial affairs. He claimed he had property worth £115000 and his debts did not exceed £64000. He estimated the value of his timber at £40000 and his stock and debts owing him to be £20000 and he declared that his financial embarrassment was due to keeping his timber unconverted and the large sum involved in running his mill business.

His blunt frankness impressed his creditors and they proposed to take some of his property to convert into cash sufficient to pay his debts. They agreed to Stares' suggestion that he managed the felling of his timber and for disposing of the rest of his property. An agreement was signed by those present and Henry Wilder and Martin Maddison, two of the creditors, were chosen as trustees. The trustees quickly found that Stares would continually obstruct their efforts in converting his assets also that the value of timber was considerably lower than Stares' estimate. In exasperation they turned to the law by bringing a commission of bankruptcy against him.

The publicity and the speed with which the assignees attempted to dispose of his property mortified Stares. He thus set about the means to stop the sale of his property by seeking wealthy friends and the political allies he had assisted in the past to help him. Some of these acquaintances were convinced that the value of Stares estates far exceeded his debts and they proposed to the assignees that eight of them would enter into an engagement to pay all the creditors their full debts plus interest if they would refrain from selling the property and relinquish the management to them. The assignees readily agreed and a deed was prepared and the assignees devolved to the new trustees their sole power of disposing of property as they thought best. The new trustees were Charles Wade, John Poore, Thomas Pink, John Ewen, Richard Palmer Baker, Hugh Digweed, Richard Lasham and

John Tredgold and the creditors were immediately paid from the pockets of these unsuspecting and eminent Hampshire businessmen.

It was not long before the trustees found great difficulties in dealing with Stares, he continued to conduct his business at an extravagant rate and again the value of his timber fell far short of his estimates. They also found that many of Stares' debts had not been declared at the time the trust was formed.

In May 1796, the trustees put the greater part of Stares' farms for sale at public auction in Botley. Stares was desperate to keep his estates and flattered himself he could do so by raising money from other yet untried friends and acquaintances. He also prevailed upon a Mr Edward Mondey, a bailiff to Governor Hornby of Hook House (near Warsash), to bid on behalf of Stares. The sale was busy and there were many bidders but Mr Mondey was the highest bidder of all. It was assumed by all that he was bidding on behalf of Mr Hornby. Uplands Farm, previously acquired dishonestly from Henry Fielder for £840 went to Mr Mondey's successful bid of £4500. Other of Stares' former estates were also knocked down to Mondey for sums far in excess of their previous value and in all Mondey's total bids amounted to £10800. The trustees were delighted that the sale of these estates had apparently brought them a greater return than they could have hoped for.

However, they were soon dismayed when they found that Mondey had been buying on behalf of Stares with money provided by yet more creditors. The trustees were mortified that they had been deceived by Stares, that the number of creditors had increased and they were soon to find that land values were decreasing.

In January 1798 they again put the estates to auction. Only two were sold, one of them in Curdridge for more than £2000 less than had been bid by Mondey. The high reserves set by the trustees discouraged buyers but were eventually sold privately at a third less than their first estimate.

Botley Mills was next on the trustees' list for disposal but once again the deviousness of Stares delayed its sale. He engaged a man named Taylor to inspect the mill under the pretence that he was acting on behalf of the Government. He alleged that the Government contemplated purchasing the mill to grind corn and bake bread for the benefit of the army. Taylor played his part in the duplicity by convincing the trustees of the Government's intentions and that Stares' son should be appointed as master miller. The trustees cherished the hope of obtaining a handsome price for the mill. When the hoax was discovered, Taylor immediately disappeared from Botley and was not seen again.

The trustees' patience with Stares was at an end and they made a final appeal to him to reveal his accounts and assist them in their aims.

PEOPLE - Robert Stares

They descended upon his house in March 1798 but he had shut himself into his bedroom alleging that he was too ill to see them. After many appeals to let them in, they broke open his door. The men surrounded his bed and they angrily accused him of his conduct and for the deceptions he had caused. Finally, a Thomas Minchin of Gosport, an attorney for the trustees and a man of Christian faith intervened. He called upon Stares to do in what little time he had left to repent and atone for all the past injuries he had done to those who surround him and others. Stares looked up and incoherently expressed his sorrow at having wronged anyone. The trustees searched his desk and found correspondence and papers that he had always denied possessing. The trustees left and it was the last meeting they had with

him. He had become depressed in body and spirit and he was taking very little food and he died on 13th April 1798.

The trustees disposed of the remaining property and the value was greatly below their expectations. The mill in particular produced only £4000 whereas the trustees had estimated it at £8000 and Stares in his original statement at £20000.

The tragedy for the worthy men who thought that they were helping a 'friend' out of a minor financial embarrassment was that they ended up out of pocket by £50000.

This biography of Robert Stares is based on an article appearing in 'The Hampshire Repository, Vol. 2' published in 1801 by an unknown author. A copy is held at the Local Studies Library, Winchester

Sherecroft looking west c.1920. Stares' home in the late 18th Century.

Photo:- Arthur Kilford Collection (HRO 59A01/14)

PEOPLE - Vice Admiral Phillip Colomb

A SUPPRESSOR OF SLAVERY

Vice Admiral Phillip Colomb

Photo.-Botley & Curdridge LHS (PH555)

Ｏne of the more interesting characters whose body resides in Botley's churchyard is Vice Admiral Phillip Howard Colomb. Colomb was born in Scotland in 1831 and after a distinguished service in the Royal Navy came in retirement to Steeple Court, Botley and died there on 13th October 1899.

Colomb entered the navy in 1846 and saw service in the China, Mediterranean and Baltic seas and active service in the Second Anglo-Burmese War (1852).and the Russian War (1855)

Colomb achieved fame and a place in naval history by perfecting a system of signalling known as Colomb's flashing signals, using a form of Morse code with long and short flashes from a lamp by night – the forerunner of the Aldis lamp. He also wrote many books particularly dealing with tactics in naval warfare, naval history and biographies.

Vice Admiral Colomb played a significant role in the suppression of the slave trade

Whilst the trading of slaves to America and Europe largely ceased in 1807, it continued unabated in the Indian Ocean as African slaves were transported by Arab merchants in dhows to the Arab States, India and China. The British Navy were despatched to the Seychelles, Aden and Bombay and other ports in the Indian Ocean to engage the traders. Colomb was to command one of the Navy ships, *H.M.S.Dryad* in 1868, and he relates his experiences in a book, *Slave Catching in the Indian Ocean* (Longmans, London.1873).

HMS Dryad

Photo—Botley & Curdridge LHS (PH556)

PEOPLE - Arthur Kilford

A VILLAGE PHOTOGRAPHER

Many of the photographs included in this publication were taken by a former Botley resident, Arthur Sidney Kilford (known as Sid). Kilford was born in 1893 in Botley. He was the son of Mr Arthur Phillip Kilford (known throughout the village as 'Chubby'), a hairdresser and his wife Elizabeth living in the High Street.

The Kilfords came from Wiltshire to Botley in 1877 when Sid's grandfather George acquired the job of stone-dresser at Botley Flour Mills and the family moved to Winchester Street and then later to the High Street in Botley.

Sid's father, Chubby had been a keen cyclist and won many trophies for cycle racing in Winchester, Eastleigh and Fareham in the 1890s. By 1895 the family had acquired the shop next to Portland House and started dealing in cycle sales and repairs.

Sid Kilford was the first apprentice to train as a motor mechanic with Hendy's, then of East Street, Southampton and later he drove as a taxi driver for Mr Harry Botting at Botley Railway Station.

Like many young men of the time, he volunteered to join the army in 1914 but was soon invalided out. After a few days at home he tried again and was accepted into the Army Service Corps, going to France as a despatch rider and later driving heavy lorries on the front line and into Germany.

After the war he returned to his father's business and also started a taxi service and ran a haulage lorry.

Kilford was a founder member of the British

Arthur Sidney Kilford 1893—1976

Photo:-By kind permission of Janet Boyd

Legion, played football for Botley and was a keen billiards player at the Men's Institute.

In the early 1900s, Sid became absorbed by the new art of photography and he captured many tranquil views of early twentieth century life in Botley.

Many of his photographs were made into postcards and many hundreds of his pictures must have been sent throughout the country. He sent some of his photographs to Germany to be colour tinted which he sold in a presentation pack of six postcards.

Sid died in 1976, aged 83 and his photographic equipment passed to his nephew, Ken Gregory.

PEOPLE - Arthur Kilford

A VILLAGE PHOTOGRAPHER

Arthur (Chubby) Kilford outside his shop in the High Street, Botley

Photo:- Arthur Kilford Collection (HRO 59A01/73)

In 1999, Ken Gregory wanted to dispose of his uncle's photographic glass negatives and donated them to the *Botley and Curdridge Local History Society*. He particularly wanted Botley villagers to appreciate their village of years past and he asked that all reproductions should acknowledge the name of the photographer.

The Society had many of Kilford's pictures copied and in March 2001 displayed them at an exhibition in the Market Hall, Botley.

To ensure safekeeping, over 500 glass plates of the Kilford collection were deposited with the Hampshire Record Office in 2001 and are held under Accession No. 59A01.

The following pages portray more of Kilford's photographs taken in the early years of the twentieth century.

PEOPLE - Arthur Kilford

A VILLAGE PHOTOGRAPHER

Arthur (Chubby) Kilford in the doorway of his Cycle shop in the High Street. 1908

Photo:- Arthur Kilford Collection (HRO 59A01/77)

High Street looking west towards Broad Oak. c.1920.

Photo:- Hampshire Record Office (63A04/B1/3/27)

PEOPLE - Arthur Kilford

A VILLAGE PHOTOGRAPHER

A typical Kilford picture showing the village celebration on the occasion of King George V's Coronation in 1911. Kilford probably used the balcony on the first floor of the shop in the High Street for this elevated view. He photographed many other street scenes from the roof of his shop at the west end of the village. Photo:- Arthur Kilford Collection (HRO 59A01/117)

Botley House in the High Street. c.1908

Photo:- Arthur Kilford Collection (HRO 59A01/45)

PEOPLE - Arthur Kilford

A VILLAGE PHOTOGRAPHER

The Elms, Outlands Lane , Curdridge Arthur Kilford Collection (HRO 59A01/19)

High Street, Botley looking north east (below). Cottages in the background were demolished in 1929 Arthur Kilford Collection (HRO 59A01/36)

PEOPLE - Arthur Kilford

A VILLAGE PHOTOGRAPHER

Godrich and Kilford's Garage at Broadoak (Now a modern Fuel Filling Station)   Photo:- Arthur Kilford Collection (HRO 59A01/118)

Celebrating the Coronation of King George V in 1911. Photograph taken from the roof of Kilford's shop looking west along the High Street

Photo:- Arthur Kilford Collection (HRO 59A01/81)

PEOPLE - Arthur Kilford

A VILLAGE PHOTOGRAPHER

Boorley Green Farm viewed from the railway bridge c.1908. The new Farm building can just be seen to the right of the former farm which was demolished shortly after this picture was taken..

Photo:- Arthur Kilford Collection (HRO 59A01/1)

Wangfield Farm—in need of restoration. c.1910

Photo:- Arthur Kilford Collection (HRO 59A01/7)

PEOPLE - John King

John King was born in 1848, the eldest son in a family of twelve. His parents resided at Yew Tree cottage in Winchester Street and his father was a sawyer and hoop maker.

He had an aptitude for learning and it was said that he was able to read simple verses at the age of 3 years. He went to a Dame school in Curdridge, as there was then no school in Botley. By the age of eight he was employed as a 'bird scarer' and then as a minder of sheep until he was fourteen. He acquired much of his education from reading while tending the sheep.

For 25 years he was a choir member at Botley church and a Sunday School teacher for 46 years.

John joined the Rifle Volunteers at the age of 16 and served for 18 years. He then became a postman but he is especially remembered for his writings of hymns and poetry.

He was the author of numerous poems dating from 1872 and composed many recruiting and war poems at the time of the first World War. His poem *'Bravo Botley—Our Lads'* captured the optimism of 1914.

Botley Square—Farewell to our Volunteers—1914

Photo — Botley and Curdridge LHS (PH222)

PEOPLE—John King

John King—The Botley Poet and Postman 1848—1923

Photo—Botley & Curdridge LHS (PH348)

We gave to our lads a ripping send off,
Who had come to their country's call,
A fine strong batch came up to the scratch,
They were just twenty-five in all.

Population? One thousand and twelve,
We may claim we are giving our share,
For now, dye ken, we have one hundred men,
Who will fight for 'The Flag' anywhere.

Folks sneeringly said our lads were afraid,

Lacked courage to come to the front;
They were 'slackers' and 'shirkers', 'loafers', 'non-workers',
Who would shrink from bearing the brunt.

False prophets they have proved everyone,
Premature, with their jeering and blame;
Their talk was all rot and the whole of the lot
Should be hanging their heads in shame.

O, gay was our street when the crowds came to greet
Our bold lads formed up in the Square
Their sisters and mothers, their sweet-hearts and brothers,
And a lot of the old 'uns were there.

The teachers and bairns from the school came down,
And they gave us a pleasant surprise,
For they not only sang our 'God Save the King',
But the Anthems of both of our Allies.

Our Rector in few but well chosen words
Then gave them 'God-speed' for us all,
And our sentiments voiced when he said he rejoiced,
They had answered Duty's stern call.

'Form fours', 'Right turn', Sergeant Kilford commands,
Then we all waved our hats as we cheered,
And we shouted aloud for we all felt so proud
For our lads who had volunteered

'Quick march' the command, and now the brass band
Breaks forth in a bold martial strain
And the vast swelling throng goes surging along
With our lads, to see them entrain

PEOPLE - John King

A right royal salute of twenty one guns,
Detonators, I ought to say,
Were fired on the line, the motive was fine,
And it heartened our lads on their way.

The train steams in, our Lads take their seats,
And the last good-byes are now said,
Now fond mother whisper 'May God bless my boy'
A like prayer ascends from each mind

They are off, and the band plays 'Auld Lang Syne'
The crowd gives them three hearty cheers,
Our true women stands and waving their hands,
They watch till the train disappears.

Ah yes, we gave them a ripping send-off,
Their hearts beat loyal and true;
But duty is plain for us who remain,
We may count it a great privilege, too.

They have left their homes and their dear ones behind,
Entrusting them all to our care,
So whate'er betide we must stand by their side
And help them their burden to bear.[21]

JOHN KING, Botley –
September,1914

All Saints Church War Memorial dedicated in 1921 commemorates the names of thirty -three men of Botley who gave their lives in the First World War and an additional twelve names added after the Second World War.

Photo:- Botley & Curdridge LHS (PH349)

21 Ethel Maffey-*John King Remembered (1989)*

PEOPLE—Jenkyns Family

Steeple Court in Church Lane, home to three generations of the Jenkyns family. The building dates from the Tudor period.

Photo:- Botley & Curdridge LHS (PH055)

Major Robin Jenkyns died in December 1981 aged sixty five. He represented the fourth and last generation of his family to live in Botley and Curdridge. The family had played a significant role in the history of both villages.

The Jenkyns family came to Botley in the 1820s when John, a lawyer, acquired Botley Hill House and other land at various times on both sides of the River Hamble. John was the second son of the Reverend John, vicar of Evercreech in Somerset, whose forebears had been clergymen in those parts for several generations before him. His two brothers were also clergymen, Henry was Canon of Durham Cathedral and Richard, Master of Balliol College, Oxford

and Dean of Wells.

John's children died in childhood and he and his wife Anna rented property in London but retained their Botley Hill home. In 1834 Botley villagers pressed for the building of a new church in the centre of the village to replace the existing church near Manor Farm. A committee was formed and as we have seen, John Jenkyns played a prominent role in the building of the new church of Botley in the 1830s.

John Jenkyns nephew, Sir Henry Jenkyns also lived at Botley Hill House and was married to Madelane Sabine Pasley the daughter of Admiral Pasley, Baronet. In

PEOPLE - Jenkyns Family

1882, Sir Henry bought the Catherine Wheel to create a Temperance Hotel and in 1884 provided much of the funds to purchase the land for Curdridge Recreation Ground and to build the Reading Room.

Arthur Jenkyns, brother of Sir Henry, lived at Coledown in Curdridge and became chairman of the Market Hall committee and Foundation Manager of Botley School. Another brother, John was Rector of Durley and when he retired he lived at Steeple Court (a former home of James Warner)

The son of John the Rector was Hugh Hobhouse Jenkyns who retired from the Indian Civil Service in the 1920s. Hugh had married Winifred Austen-Leigh, a relation of Jane Austen.

Arguably one of the greatest deeds of the Jenkyns family was Hugh Jenkyns' intervention into the intended sale of building plots along the east side of the River Hamble. As mentioned elsewhere, he and his wife acquired land which he donated to the National Trust and ensured protection along much of the Upper Hamble river against development.

Hugh Jenkyns died in a shooting accident on his estate at Botley in 1948. His widow continued to live at Steeple Court until her death in 1973.

PEOPLE - Dr Alfred Pern

Alfred Spearman Pern was born in Botley in 1887 the son of Dr and Mrs Alfred Pern.

After medical training, Dr Pern joined his father's general practice in Botley in 1910 and eventually took over when his father died in 1914.

The Practice covered a very wide area which included Hamble, Bursledon and Hedge End as well as Botley and Curdridge and he travelled by bicycle in his early days before acquiring firstly a motor cycle and then a car.

On the death of his father, Dr Pern became Medical Officer of Health for the South Stoneham Guardians until 1925 when the Poor Law Union was transferred to the Southampton Guardians. He was also the Honourable Medical Officer of Health for the Winchester Rural District Council, Medical Officer of the former Shedfield Cottage Hospital and Chairman of the Southampton branch of the British Medical Association.

He was connected with the Botley and Curdridge Nurses Home since the early days when it was concerned with the provision of a District Nurse. He was a member of the House Committee and its Medical Officer and at the time of his death was Honourable Secretary and Trustee. Dr Pern was also the administrative trustee for the Burrell and Penfold Charities.

Dr Pern followed his father as Church Warden at All Saints Church, Botley, an office his father had held for 33 years and apart from brief intervals in the war years, Dr Pern held this position until his death. He

was Botley's representative on Diocesan and Deanery committees and took a special interest in administration and finance.

Dr.Alfred Pern 1887-1970

Photo:-Botley & Curdridge LHS (PH559)

He was a man of many talents, which included hand embroidery, bell ringing and stamp collecting.

During the First World War he was a Major in the 4th Battalion of the Hampshire Regiment T.A. and as Colonel in the Second World War he was in charge of a Casualty Clearing Station of the British General Hospital and was awarded the OBE. Dr

PEOPLE - Dr Alfred Pern

Pern held office in the Botley British Legion and regularly led the annual parade of ex-servicemen in the local Remembrance Day services.

In February 1922 he was awarded the Médaille du Roi Albert in recognition of the devotion shown to works of charity in connection with the Belgian Refugee committee at the Port of Southampton.

In 1915 he married Miss Grace Oakes, daughter of the Rev. and Mrs Oakes of the Vicarage, Netley Marsh. All of their married life was spent in Botley and they had four sons, Paul, John, Tom and Christopher.

The Doctor and his wife had been connected with Botley Choral Society since its inception and he became its President. Dr Pern was Hon. Secretary of the Curdridge and Botley Horticultural Society and a member of the South Hants Farmers Club.

Chairman of Botley Parish Council for nine years after the Second World War, Dr Pern had been a School Manager and chairman of the Boy Scout group at Botley, President of the Botley Pensioners' Association and for over 55 years a Trustee of both the ancient Order of Foresters and the Oddfellow Friendly Societies.

A keen local historian, he was actively interested in the preservation of beauty spots, especially on the River Hamble.

Dr Pern retired from General Practice in 1958 and died in September 1970.

THE POOR HOUSE

Oak Tree Cottage, Hedge End. Botley's former Poor House

Photo:-Botley & Curdridge LHS (CPIC0077)

Before workhouses were built every parish owned a few cottages which were used to accommodate the poor. For the most part these were little better than hovels, damp and insanitary, with just one room and a ladder giving access to the roof space. Parishes also provided clothing, fuel and relief in cash.

Botley provided a Poor House at the end of the eighteenth century on the edge of the common land, in what is now Hedge End. It comprised a brick and tiled cottage with detached bakehouse, woodshed, piggeries and an area of land about 1.5 acres at the rear of the Wheatsheaf Public House. This public house was in Upper Northam Road and was demolished in the early years of the twentieth century.

The first reference to the Poor House appears in the Botley Vestry minutes of 15th April 1818, when the meeting elected a new Master and Mistress to the Poor House to replace Benjamin Burroughs and his wife. It is not clear what the former Master and his wife had done wrong but they were 'discharged'.[22]

The new Masters were John Ashwyn and his wife from Southampton *'they having brought with them a satisfactory character'*. Their salary was to be £15 per annum and they are to be supplied with board and lodging for themselves and one child consisting of the same provision as the

THE POOR HOUSE

paupers were allowed in the House. *'They shall also set to work all paupers that are capable and those as cannot work abroad should be supplied with work within the House'*

Also *'That should the paupers who prove disrespectful to the Master or disobedient to the rules of the House, should be put upon bread and water and if that is not found sufficient that they should instantly be taken before the Magistrate'*.

A rate was set of 2 shillings (10p) in the pound was made for the relief of the poor.

In 1819 the Vestry agreed a rate of £15 per annum to Mr Robert Swann, Surgeon, to attend all paupers who live within 5 miles and attend all mid-wifery cases at 12d (5p) each per head.

In 1820 the Vestry resolved that *'a double cottage should be erected in the cheapest manner possible viz. clay and wattle and a brick chimney consisting of a room 12 ft (3.65mtrs.) square and a double bedroom to each situated in the plot of ground adjacent to the existing Work House'*.

It was in 1826 that the Vestry considered placing the Parish with other adjoining parishes, *'to establish a House of Industry for the reception, maintenance and employment of the whole of the poor who are now or may hereinafter become chargeable upon the rates of the several Parishes'*.

The Poor Law Amendment Act of 1834 superseded the need for parishes to provide a poorhouse. The act stopped external relief for the poor leaving those unfortunates with the choice of the workhouse or starvation. The workhouse separated husbands and wives and parents from children. They were forced to stay apart and not even permitted to meet in communal places such as the chapel. Men and children would be expected to do heavy work in the workhouse and women worked long hours washing and cleaning or other tasks for a bowl of gruel and a piece of bread.

The South Stoneham Union Workhouse was built in West End (now Moorgreen Hospital) in 1835, to where Botley's poor were sent.

Botley's Poor House was subsequently sold and the funds received transferred to the South Stoneham Union. The cottage remained a private property until it was demolished in the 1960s.

HOUSES

Steeple Court. c.1920

Photo:- Botley & Curdridge LHS (PH306)

Botley and Curdridge contain several large fine houses some surviving from the Elizabethan period such as the 1610 jettied house in Winchester Street and Steeple Court in Church Lane

It is believed that **Steeple Court** was first built in about 1600 for the walls are built using Tudor bricks. A major reconstruction took place in about 1750 when most of the windows were replaced by larger windows to provide considerably more light.

Until 1884 Steeple Court was in the area of land belonging to the Parish of Droxford. This extended along the River Hamble from Horsepool by Botley Quay in the north to Dock Copse in the south.

It was the home of James Warner in 1833 when he bought the Manor of Botley. Warner died in 1858 and the family remained at Steeple Court until the end of the nineteenth century. It then became the home of the Jenkyns family. More recently it has been owned by Mr and Mrs J Firth.

HOUSES

Sherecroft c.1920

Photo:- Arthur Kilford Collection (HRO 59A01/3)

General in Wellington's army at Waterloo; William Cobbett who rented the house from Kempt between 1812 and 1817; Richard Chevenix Trench, first curate of Curdridge's Chapel of Ease and Canon Maltby, father in law of Vice Admiral Barry.

Brook House is on the east side of Brook Lane near its junction with Southampton Road. The nineteenth-century house has been extended in recent years to make it suitable for the needs of Woodhill School. A new Masonic Hall was built to the rear of the house. The first known owner was William Warner, son of James Warner. Subsequent owners were Major General Walter Henry Smith and family, John Lewis Langworthy, and in 1894 it was purchased by Beckett Burton Powell. Beckett Powell was born in 1853 and went to Argentina in 1870 to work for the Buenos Aires Great Southern Railway. As a surveyor

Earlier members of the Jenkyns' family lived at **Botley Hill House** on the Curdridge side of the River Hamble opposite Botley Mills. This was the home of John Jenkyns in the 1830s, who was a lawyer and responsible for organising the building of All Saints church. Previously it was the residence of a former Lord of the Manor, Rev Richard Eyre.

Opposite on the north side of the Botley to Curdridge road is Sherecroft built in the late eighteenth century. **Sherecroft House** stood on the site of a former farm known in its early days as Botley Hill Farm. The infamous Robert Stares came to live at the farm with his parents in 1744 and it is probable that the building now known as Sherecroft was built for Stares.   Stares owned many other farms in Botley and Curdridge and was a tenant of Botley Mills.

Other owners included Sir James Kempt, a

HOUSES

Brook House c.1930

Photo:-By kind permission of Brian Powell

he planned many of their routes. Powell died in 1929 and his widow, Elizabeth sold the house in 1934 to William George Miller, a trainer of greyhounds.

Beckett Powell had 'Woodlands' (now called **'Gould Copse'**) in Brook Lane built for his sister, Charlotte and her husband Richard Haines Little for his retirement.

The original **Kitnocks House** in Curdridge dates from the sixteenth century but was totally destroyed by fire at the end of the nineteenth century. It is said that the first building was built of flint and stood like a castle with a moat and drawbridge. The earliest record of the estate gave the name of the owner as Knox, a gentleman who had a very beautiful daughter named Kate. It was this daughter who gave the name to the

residence as Kitnocks and, it is said, Kitty's ghost frequents Kitnocks Hill at midnight!

The legend tells that Kitty Knox had a suitor who did not find favour with her father and so their meetings were in secret. One day Kitty was missing from home and a search revealed her dead body in the moat. It was thought that she had committed suicide but it was proved later that she had been trying to cross the moat to join her lover when she slipped and drowned as she was attempting to elope with him.

The hill later became known as Kitnocks Hill and people often said they saw her there but without her head!

HOUSES

One of Kitnocks' last residents before the fire destroyed the original house was Henry Liddell, Dean of Christ Church, Oxford, whose daughter Alice was famously to become the inspiration for Alice in Wonderland for Lewis Carroll .

In 1948 following the death of Major Charles Randolph, owner of Kitnocks from 1904, the house was sold to Hampshire County Council and in 1993 it was acquired privately and run as a private nursing home.

Gould Copse, Brook Lane c.1920

Photo:- Arthur Kilford Collection (HRO 59A01/15)

Kitnocks House in 2007

Photo:- DH Stokes

STRAWBERRY TRADE

Strawberry growing commenced in central southern Hampshire in the mid nineteenth century. The mild climatic conditions and soil of the area were such that it became for a time the largest strawberry growing region in Europe.

The trade attracted many growers with small landholdings of between one and three acres and there were at least 36 commercial growers in Botley by the 1930s.

It was a risky business for a market of only six to seven weeks a year. Growers had to make enough money in that time to provide for their families for a year. Frosts, lack of sun or rain and disease all posed threats to a successful crop.

The majority of local crops were despatched throughout the British mainland from Botley railway station and would reach markets and shops the day after picking. On 29th June 1923 it was reported that over 66000 baskets of strawberries were despatched by rail from Botley in 64 freight vans. To accommodate the increased strawberry traffic extra sidings were built at the station where Yeoman's Processing Plant now stands. In the early mornings of the

Loading strawberry baskets at Botley Station.

Photo:- Arthur Kilford Collection (HRO 59A01/64)

STRAWBERRY TRADE

Strawberry pickers on a market garden in Botley

Photo:- Arthur Kilford Collection (HRO 59A01/106)

strawberry season a queue of horses and carts stretched from the station yard and into Station Road. It was this traffic, and the need of the horses, which made the erection of the drinking fountain at the station entrance such a practical memorial for Queen Victoria's golden jubilee.

After the Second World War, competition from Spain and Italy brought about a rapid decline of the English strawberry industry.

Modern methods of strawberry cultivation have been pioneered in Botley. In the 1970s, one grower introduced black polythene mulch on raised beds in lieu of straw to protect plants from damp, disease and weeds. Clear polythene tunnels were used to protect the plants from frost and bad weather with straw used between the beds to protect the fruit from 'soil splash'.

More recently, another Botley grower introduced 'growbags' at table height to provide ease of picking, improve air circulation and to control irrigation and feeding thus giving a greater yield.

Nowadays, strawberries consigned to supermarkets, are delivered to warehouses where they are chilled and packaged and distributed to retailers – three to four days after picking. A far cry from overnight delivery nearly a century ago!

THE NURSES TRUST

Augusta Burrell was born in Durham in 1839 the daughter of a wealthy mine owner. With her brother, Robert Anthony Burrell JP, they came to live at Fairthorne Manor in 1879. Augusta was a devout Christian and used her wealth for the benefit of all: the church; local hospitals; Red Cross; servicemen from the war in France; Titanic Disaster fund; local clubs and Societies. Many others all benefitted from her generosity.

In 1867,[23] the wife of the Botley Rector, the Rev. John Morley Lee started a public subscription to support the employment of a nurse in Botley and Curdridge. A nurse was appointed but it later became a struggle to keep the subscriptions flowing. Augusta Burrell came to support the fund and she also gave £400 towards the founding of a Nurses Cottage Home for Botley and Curdridge providing that a similar sum was raised by the Parishes and other sources. Part of the additional money was acquired from the Botley War Relief Fund, a fund started in 1915 to assist local men disabled during the war. Leehurst, a cottage in the High Street opposite the Primary School, was purchased with this money in 1921 and was to become the Nurses Home for the next 47 years. A plaque was added to the cottage wall stating:-

Dedicated to the Memory

Of the men of

Botley and Curdridge

Who fell in the Great War

1914-1918

The Trustees of the Botley and Curdridge Nurses Home consisted of the Rector, a representative of both Parish Councils and elected members from both villages.

Following the introduction of the National Health Service in 1948, Leehurst was leased to Hampshire County Council on condition that the house should only be used as a residence for a District Nurse.

However, in 1968, the Trustees were informed by the Hampshire County Council Social Services that a previous Act of Parliament placed the responsibility upon the County Council for providing a District Nurse with a house to live in. As such it took away the main purpose for which the Trust was created. Also at the time, Leehurst was unoccupied because it needed urgent modernisation and the Trust were unable to raise sufficient funds to finance the work. For these reasons the Trust requested the Charity Commissioners to sanction the sale of Leehurst.

This they did and the house was sold for £3707-17s-0d and the proceeds given to the official Custodian of Charitable Funds for investment.

Because Leehurst was also a memorial to those killed in the 1914-1918 war, it was decided to create a memorial garden adjacent to Leehurst. This land was bought by the Parish Council for £50 and on it was erected a public seat with a shelter wall. The memorial plaque was removed from the wall of the house and mounted on the seat shelter.

THE NURSES TRUST

The investment from the sale of the house and accumulated trust fund is used for the sick and poor of Botley and Curdridge. A yearly report of such payment is given at each village's annual parish meeting.

Trustee members at the unveiling of the memorial seat in the garden adjacent to Leehurst L .to R. The Rector, the Reverend Colin Wheatley, Vi Cooke, Mrs Nicholas, Mrs Shave, Mr Reeves-Rowland and Mrs Boswell.

Photo—Botley & Curdridge LHS (PH349)

MURDER ON THE HIGHWAY

July 1799 saw the arrival to barracks in Botley of His Majesty's Loyal Tarbert Regiment of Fencibles Infantry. The Tarbert Fencibles, as they were known, were formed by Sir Edward Leslie MP of Tarbert in County Kerry and provided a service for George III. The Regiment was ordered to Botley to provide part of the defence against a possible French invasion.

The Fencibles numbered 480 men and were accompanied by nearly 500 women and their children. They had travelled for six months from their homes in the south west of Ireland, almost entirely on foot. On the way they suffered many hardships including the death of 80 men, women and children when a lighter capsized on a river in Ireland.

They were not entirely welcomed at Botley. It is probable that they encamped on Botley Common though many were housed with residents for it is recorded that a halfpenny a day was paid for quartering a soldier. Thieving, poaching, drunkenness and brawling were commonplace. However, there were happier occasions when Ann Hilman of Botley married one of the soldiers and one of the Regiment's women, Catherine Breen married Edmund Brown, a local man.

On Tuesday 11th February 1800, 70 year old Thomas Webb of Swanmore, a peddlar of woodenware was returning home after buying eggs in Botley. As he approached Curdridge Common, Webb was attacked by two men and severely beaten and thrown into a ditch. The attackers stole the eggs and what little money he had, said to be as little as 7d(3p). Despite his injuries, Webb crawled from the ditch and somehow made his way across the common to the cottage of Daniel Barfoot in Outlands Lane. Half conscious, in intense pain and covered with blood and dirt he was helped into the cottage. The Barfoots were horrified to see, rammed into his neck, the broken stump of an army bayonet six inches in length. The doctor was summoned who removed the bayonet and provided what help he could but Webb was soon to die.

Memorial stone to the cruel murder of an old man on Curdridge Common

Photo—Botley & Curdridge LHS (PH287)

MURDER ON THE HIGHWAY

The incriminating bayonet was sent to the officers of the Tarbert Fencibles and they were told that their men were suspected of murder. Captain Godfrey Massey's investigation revealed that men were missing from barracks at the time of the attack and his enquiries led to the arrest of Privates John Diggon and Richard Prendergast and Sergeant James Collopy.

On the following Saturday the Tarbert Fencibles marched from Botley to new barracks in Winchester, possibly as a routine posting or perhaps in deference to the people of Botley.

The three men were committed to trial at the Lent Assizes at Winchester Castle on 4th March 1800. There Private Diggon was convicted of the murder and sentenced to death, Sergeant Collopy and Private Prendergast were acquitted. Prendergast, although acquitted by the Court, was accused by the Army of disobedience and a court marshal sentenced him to 1000 lashes and to be drummed out of the army.

John Diggon went to the gallows in Winchester on the 10th March. He confessed to another robbery near Botley and he begged pardon of this victim and of Thomas Webb's widow. In accordance with his sentence, Diggon's body was suspended in chains on a gibbet at Curdridge Common near the spot where the murder was committed. It is said that his remains hung in chains for forty years before the Common Warden, William Hickey, buried his bones.

This murder is recorded with a memorial stone erected originally near to the scene of the crime by the present railway entrance. The railway was built in 1841 and the memorial was moved to King's Corner. When the road here was realigned many years ago the stone was again removed and finally relayed next to the horse drinking fountain at the entrance to Botley railway station, near to its original position. The stone became indecipherable and has been replaced by a cast iron version. The stone memorial is still there behind the cast plate but is partly hidden under overgrowing ivy. The memorial is inscribed *'This Stone is Erected to Perpetuate a Most Cruel Murder Commited on the Body of Thomas Webb a Poor Inhabitant of Swanmore on the 11 of February 1800 by John Diggins a Private Soldier In the Talbot Fencibles Whose remains are Gibbeted on the adjoining Common'.* The memorial contains two errors – Diggins and Talbot should read Diggon and Tarbert.

GUY FAWKES CELEBRATION

Botley Square, November 1931

Shortly after the First World War, it became a tradition in Botley to celebrate Guy Fawkes Day with a huge bonfire in the Square. Each year the fire became bigger and the young men of the village found more and more dubious sources of fuel for the fire. It also caused concern to the occupants of the properties around the Square.

However, in November 1926, it was reported in the *Hampshire Chronicle*: *"Although it was decided to abandon the annual bonfire demonstration this year, a fire was lit in the Market Square. The proceedings were on a much smaller scale than in former years out of consideration for the fuel shortage and in order that valuable wood should not be wasted."*

Perhaps not unconnected with this report, the *Hampshire Chronicle* in its same issue quotes the Botley Rector who asked *"I should be grateful if the public would try to prevent the rapid disappearance of what was once the Rectory fence--"* !!

The bonfire celebrations continued with greater intensity in subsequent years. In 1927 an old cart and motor tyres were used to fuel the fire. A year later it was reported *"The fuel for the fire consisted of all manner of items, much being provided in the usual unauthorised way. The fire raged until late in the evening and was finally put out by the local fireman. But did the excited band who attempted to re-start the fire expect the drenching they received when the firemen played the hose on them?"*

GUY FAWKES CELEBRATION

Eight young men were arrested on this occasion and appeared at the Eastleigh Bench and were each fined 5 shillings (25p) for doing wilful damage to a barrel of tar belonging to South Stoneham Rural District Council. One of the boys, Alfred Elliott, remarked there were some 80 boys concerned and only 8 of them had been 'pinched' for it !!

Our picture shows the result of the bonfire in 1931 where the *Hampshire Chronicle* reported *'A huge crowd gathered in the Market Square on Guy Fawkes evening, apparently anticipating that the old tradition of lighting a large bonfire in the Square would not be allowed to drop. All doubts were banished about 10-30, then a burning barrel appeared in the Square, this being the signal that the fun was about to begin.*

Quantities of old motor tyres and bundles of wood soon made a blaze, to say nothing of tins of grease and numerous articles which were thrown on the flames. Then amid cheers from the crowds, a motor car appeared from somewhere and many strong hands had soon run it into the centre of the fire. The fun continued until the early hours of the morning, when the crowd began to disperse. A heap of debris and twisted iron etc. was to be seen in the centre of the Square for several days'

The fence around the policeman's house in the High Street was caught alight during the bonfire of 1933 and thereafter it is believed that celebrations were a little less spectacular.

PLANE CRASH AT CURDRIDGE

Aircraft Crash in the grounds of Furzecote, Curdridge

Photo:-Botley & Curdridge LHS (PH553)

In the early hours of the morning of the 16th September, 1926 a twin engine Handley Page HP24 (Hydrabad) Aircraft was on a night flight from Kings Lynn in Norfolk to Gosport when it crashed into a garden in Upper Curdridge.

Four aircraft, from No.99 Squadron, were on the night flight when one of the HP24s developed engine trouble and, descending in thick fog, hit some tall trees and crashed into the grounds of *Furzecote*.

Miss Smith who lived in the cottage near the scene of the crash, telephoned for an ambulance and also called Dr Pern of Botley who was quickly at the incident.

A large crowd of helpers gathered around the wrecked aircraft and the injured men were quickly removed. There was a leakage of fuel and several small outbreaks of fire which were promptly extinguished. It was later reported that the aircraft had about 300 gallons of fuel on board and it was fortunate that the tanks were not ruptured during the accident

Two of the four crewmen were seriously injured with ankle and hip fractures and were removed to Haslar Hospital for treatment. The two other members of the crew suffered minor back injuries and scratches.

BOTLEY ELECTION RIOT

A general election was held on the 1st of December 1885 and polling took place at the National School (Botley Primary School). Botley was in the Fareham Division of the South Hampshire constituency. At about 6-30 on that evening, a mob of young men from Hedge End and Bursledon entered the Square shouting abuse, throwing stones at residents and property and, without provocation, knocking villagers to the ground and rolling them in the mud. Many of the tradesmen's plate glass windows were smashed and most of the properties in the High Street and Winchester Street suffered broken windows. Portland Villa, the home of Mr William Harding, was thought to have been the Conservative Committee room and was a particular target of the mob, though Liberal houses were also damaged.

The mob turned their attention to the polling station and attempted to enter the school building to remove the ballot box. Officials and the two policemen on duty barricaded themselves in and prevented the removal of the box. It is reported that the Presiding Officer, Mr Leonard Warner, eventually left the building with the ballot box, unseen by

Portland House 2007. In 1885 it was the home of William Harding and used as a Committee Room for the Conservative Party at the General Election.

Photo:- DH Stokes

the attackers, and made for the railway across fields and reached Botley station by walking along the track.

Telegrams were sent to Bitterne and Winchester for police assistance but none arrived that evening and the mob were in control of the village until they dispersed at about 10-30pm.

A month later, at the Southampton County Bench, James Hopkins, John Hopkins, Henry Hopkins, Samuel Othen, Richard Jurd, Daniel Barfoot, Harry Wellstead, James Lebbern and William Sharp, were charged by the police for rioting in Botley and they were committed for trial at the Winchester Quarter Sessions.

Some days after the court case, a principal witness against the above accused men, a Mr William Pearce, a gardener in the employ of Mr William Harding, was drinking in the Three Horse Shoes public house in Botley when he was attacked from behind by James George Bailey. Witnesses to the attack said that there was clearly some ill-feeling about the rioting case. Bailey admitted knocking the complainant's hat off and was fined 5shillings (25p) plus costs.

At the Quarter Sessions in Winchester,[24] the above nine accused men plus William Earwicker, Henry Emery and John Ryves were found guilty on six charges of causing a riot, casting stones and brickbats, unlawful assembly, assault on certain persons and damage to property. The accused were found guilty and were imprisoned and kept to hard labour for one calendar month.

The reason for the riot is not clear. It is generally believed that animosity existed particularly between Hedge End and Botley villagers in the nineteenth century. This was probably due to the perception by Hedge End people that Botley was not of 'their class'. Botley was a prosperous village that included many residents of 'gentlemen' status including retired military and naval officers and skilled tradesmen. Hedge End on the other hand was emerging on the former Botley Common with no more than very basic housing. This rivalry between the villages continued into the twentieth century on a more civilised basis when contests such as tug of war (across the River Hamble), 'It's a knockout' and football competitions were held.

Newspapers reporting this riot also contained news of minor disturbances and hooliganism in Wickham, Fareham, Titchfield, Worthing and other towns on the occasion of the election day in 1885. This particular election was the first in which all men over the age of 21 were allowed to vote but no reason can be found for these acts of lawlessness.

WORLD WAR II

During World War II, Botley remained largely unscathed from enemy action but there is still some evidence today of the defensive measures constructed in the village and of the preparations for the D Day offensive.

In the early months of the war, the RAF established a decoy site near Marks Farm. The site was intended to replicate the Northam area of Southampton, the curve in the Hamble River being similar to that of the River Itchen. The site consisted of a control building linked to a series of large bonfire sites. After the first enemy bombers had passed over, the fires were ignited and the Luftwaffe was then tempted into bombing southern Botley rather than the heavily populated and industrialised Northam. This probably had some effect because a string of seven High Explosive bombs fell very close to the decoy site and Marks Farm.

Anti-tank concrete blocks were erected in the Square and along the boundary walls of Sherecroft. Also built into this wall at the eastern end was a pillbox (a defensive machine gun enclosure). Anderson air raid shelters were constructed in gardens and it was reported that 86 Morrison Shelters were also issued to some villagers for those who needed bomb protection inside their homes.

Air raid precautions throughout the Country were strictly enforced and there is ample evidence that there were lapses in Botley. There were many instances at Eastleigh Police Court of residents being fined for showing lights after dark. One incident refers to a motor cyclist who ran into a herd of cows in Holmesland Lane. The herdsman, John Rowe, pleaded guilty and was fined 10 shillings (50p) for driving animals during darkness without a dimmed white light in front and behind the herd and the owner of the cattle was fined 7/6d (37½ p). Another resident, a woman from Church Lane, was also fined 10 shillings for showing a light during the night – she pleaded guilty explaining she had had a very worrying time as she had 5 sons in the army.

A more serious event occurred in June 1941 when a farm on the outskirts of the village received a direct hit and 5 people were killed.

As D Day approached, the village saw a massive build up of British, American and

Command Post for Decoy Site near Marks Farm. c.1942

Photo:- Botley & Curdridge LHS (PH097)

WORLD WAR II

Canadian servicemen and service vehicles, jeeps, tanks and personnel carriers. The vehicles were parked along many of the roads in Botley and, in Maddoxford Lane, lay-bys were specially constructed to accommodate tanks.

A large tented camp was created at Fairthorne Manor for Canadian troops and the Manor itself became the headquarters for directing the Canadian assault on Normandy.

HMS Cricket Camp was constructed in 1943 as a Royal Naval shore establishment in preparation for the invasion of Europe. The camp comprised 120 individual buildings, including a NAAFI (Navy, Army & Air Force Institute created by the Government to provide recreational establishments at military centres) with a cinema, a small hospital and an extensive complex of Nissen accommodation huts surrounding central ablution facilities. An armament depot and a sewerage works suitable for a small town were also constructed, all served by a network of roads. The Hoe Moor Creek (off the Hamble River) was dredged and widened to give access to about a dozen docking bays to moor landing craft. Three large country houses, across the creek in Bursledon, *Brixedone, Durncombe* and *Freehills* were requisitioned to provide Officers' and WRENs' accommodation.

It was on the night of 5th June 1944, that the craft moved down the Hamble River to begin the epic invasion of Europe.

Cricket Camp was decommissioned by the Admiralty in July 1945 and the site became home to returning servicemen and for those who had lost their homes due to enemy bombing.

Relics of this war time establishment– the guardhouse (as you enter Manor Farm Country Park), the outlines of the mooring bays and the foundations of the huts can still be seen today.

The men and women who served at HMS Cricket are remembered in a memorial erected in the Country Park which was unveiled by the Countess Mountbatten in June 2004.

I take this opportunity of again thanking all those people who have so willingly given of their time, knowledge and expertise in the production of this book.

಄಄಄಄಄

The *Botley and Curdridge Local History Society* was formed in 1972 to encourage an interest in local history and to collect, record and preserve items of local interest. The records are kept in a Society Archive and meetings are held throughout the year at the Diamond Jubilee Hall, Botley

಄಄಄಄಄

In October 2011. the Society merged with the *Durley History Society* creating the *Botley Curdridge and Durley History Society*

Dennis Stokes